VOYAGE IN DESTINY

Part four — The return to true knowledge

Francesco Alessandrini

Udine – Italy – 2011

authorHOUSE®

AuthorHouse™ UK Ltd.
500 Avebury Boulevard
Central Milton Keynes, MK9 2BE
www.authorhouse.co.uk
Phone: 08001974150

First published by AuthorHouse 5/5/2011

ISBN: 978-1-4567-7779-1 (sc)
ISBN: 978-1-4567-7780-7 (e)

Original title:
Viaggio nel destino – Quarta parte –
Il ritorno alla vera conoscenza.

Translation from Italian by:
Paul Rinaldi – Udine – Italy – 2010

Contents

Thanks...

This book is not mine, without the will of the Masters it would never have existed.

My first and huge thanks is for their authorship. I owe them a lot and certainly not only for this book. Without A and B this book would never have seen the light, my thanks and affection to them goes beyond all limits, thanks also to Tebor, the 'Goddess of encounter', who allowed me to meet A and B.

Thanks to Maddalena, my sweet partner, for her uncommon patience in supporting me in this adventure.

I also thank all the authors who I read some of the pieces of this text to, these reading allowed me to quickly access certain knowledge of the Masters and to have enough confirmation from their help not to consider myself a madman.

Preface.

Every one of us has a destiny.

It contains a series of causes and connections that not even the most fervid imagination could visualize.

Generally we do not notice destiny, but, if we are able to interpret and listen to things which happen to us, at times we can pick up signs which try to align us to it.

In the end destiny unfolds itself even if we willingly oppose it. It is better to try and follow it without creating too many obstacles on the way.

That is exactly what I am trying to do here.

Writing this book is part of my destiny, which I do not claim to be "grandiose".

Maybe the credit should go to Who gave the initial spark to my soul, maybe the credit should also go to me for the quality and quantity of work I have developed.

I am certain, however, that the credit should also go to those Invisible Helpers which Life has put at our disposal.

By reading the following, you will have a way of knowing Them and thanking Them.

This book partially talks about my destiny, more so it is an investigation into the lives of us all and life in general, it is an attempt to discover how Life interacts between humans and the Universe, but above all, I want to indicate a road of return to "real knowledge", or moreover to the knowledge of " the real ", overcoming the barriers of illusion in which, unfortunately, in this age we are immersed.

This book follows other three other books of the same title:

"Voyage in destiny – first part – A private diary."
"Voyage in destiny – second part – The diary of the development of my public story."
"Voyage in destiny – third part – From the analysis of certain ancient discoveries, a message for the survival of mankind."

At the moment of writing they have not been published yet.

In the first two books I have gathered the pages of a diary in which I talk about a small but great morsel of a voyage in destiny, and not only mine.

They contain the first part of a fantastic experience I had between the end of 2006 and the first half of 2009.

I had the chance to meet a Master of Light, a spiritual entity of the highest level on an almost weekly basis. This gave me an understanding that life on Earth as we know it is nothing more than a small subset of an immensely and incredibly more significant and larger phenomenon.

In the *first part* I spoke about the initial phases of the adventure, on the sense, the mechanisms and the meaning of life that the Masters allowed me to know along the way. That *"first part"* is supported by many of my real life situations and of those of friends and acquaintances, this is the reason I have summarily indicated the story in which it is told as "private".

The *second part*, although temporally intersected with the first, talks about the beginning and initial development of a "public" story. By this I mean that its contents do not only regard me or people close to me but about the destiny of the entire human race. It is the development of a voyage of gradual rediscovery of a knowledge that regards mankind, but that is not human.

In both parts I was helped by two dear friends, A and B, two very special people.

B does energy therapy; we could define him as a " therapeutist of the soul", while A, his wife, is capable of writing what the Master of Light tells her. Just ask a question and thanks to her a reply is given from the Spirit World.

In the third part of *"Voyage in destiny"*, I did not seek out the sustained help of A and B to let mankind understand that its vision of reality is not complete and, at times, incorrect. As long as mankind thinks only as a human being it will never achieve the Knowledge.

An opening to something deeper is necessary, something more true, less apparent and illusionary, as is mankind's normal interpretation of life.

In order to arrive at a correct interpretation of Life, the Spiritual point of view has to enter mankind as it did in ancient times.

The way to understand this, in the *third book*, is through an analysis, sometimes detailed, sometimes less so, of three ancient discoveries.

The analysis leads to an almost completely new interpretation of their meaning, so much so, that after initial attempts to compare it to already noted learning, I threw in the towel and proceeded along a new and unexpected trail.

This *fourth book* goes on from the other three examining their ideas and arguments in more detail.

Its aim is to bring you and me back to the "true knowledge" or at least to the path of "true knowledge". I say bring back because, in effect, we are talking about a "return" to a knowledge already known to mankind who walked on Earth's fertile soil a long time ago.

This knowledge got lost and now we have reached the moment of renewal after thousands of years of oblivion.

The narrative is very complex and I certainly have no pretentions to exhaust it in this book, although I believe this discussion is an important detail in the knowledge of an infinite reality.

This book is no different from all the others I am writing, in as much as the style and the things I write are those that I am given to understand at the moment. I know for certain that the successive steps on the path of knowledge can only be made when the previous ones have been understood and every single argument is subject to this logic of learning. You can therefore find arguments already dealt with in previous books, but with the added aspect that represents a forward move I have made in arriving at a more complete understanding.

It is my personal "state of the art" of knowledge.

I know that I still have a lot to examine and learn but I have the presumption to think that a lot has already been done.

For those who appreciate only the teaching of human sciences this book will seem to be the fruit of madness. Its reading will often provoke an incredulous sense of negation and they will immediately go back to their reassuring teachings.

This is expected to happen.

However, for those who are open to evaluate a perspective that does not come from that generated by habits of the physical world, a new and interesting chapter could be opened in their lives.

A wish for the readers.

I hope that this strange book stimulates a desire in you to abandon the arrogance which insists that thoughts generated by the human mind are the only ones possible; now is the time to be open to a wider thought, from a High and Other provenance.

Some indications for reading.

I have tried, wherever possible, to use a simple and popular language.

However, on re-reading I notice that I have taken a set of knowledge that I have learned for granted. This has been learned over the years in places out with the common and not used in, or sensitive to practical life that we all have to face.

A specific knowledge also comes from my profession and mentality as an engineer.

My way of solving problems, which I call "enjoyment", is to go straight to the crux of the matter and thus maybe ignoring certain steps in explaining myself to others.

I say the above to excuse myself if some of the statements that you come across are limited in their comprehension, they are products of my experience and cultural background, which do not always come out explicitly.

Maybe you will have already noticed that sometimes I use the word "Masters" and other times "Master". In fact, I do not know if who is helping me are Masters or if there is only one, or if they are called by another name ... it is a voice from someone and from a place that I do not know well, yet.

The only thing I know for certain is that I can no longer keep the infinite profundity of that voice to myself.

The assertions of the Masters.

One thing which had me bewildered from the start, was the unknown in the verifiable objectivity in the assertions of the Masters.

We are used to considering things "objectively" in relation to how they happen in our physical reality. We admire and have faith in anyone who can predict the realization of something which then actually happens, but we tend to lose faith if someone tells us something which does not happen in the physical world.

Well, the Masters do not follow this logic.

Some of their predictions, no matter how strange or absurd, have happened punctually.

At other times they have predicted or asserted things which immediately seem incredible or even really opposed to good sense, and which did not happen.

What should we think then?

I can only say that they do not follow normal human logic.

The Masters see much more than just life on Earth.

They have a much wider perspective than ours.

Their vision is spatial, temporal and inter-dimensional, it is not finalized on physical events but on something more profound. Basically, they are always searching for the maximum well-being of our souls and sometimes they force us to think and act in absurd ways to realize this.

This way of appealing to and acting on our "mental state" will have a consequent effect on our behaviour thus making things move in the best possible direction for us without damaging the situation of others. It is not easy to square such a state of things to our normal way of thinking, resistance is huge.

Deep faith in the Masters is the only way which can make us accept this, a real and true faith capable of overcoming every appearance and every absurdity. Without doing so, we will remain trapped within the limits of human logic nonetheless influenced and guided by superior "threads" without ever being able to understand their existence or the direction in which they move.

"Faith" is the key word which will open another vision of things for us.

Naturally, we have to be very careful in who we put our faith in, but that is another question.

I say this because a large part of what I have to tell you was "obtained" and defined by methods which certainly cannot be defined as scientific even if, all things considered, logical.

The analysis was often passed on by the Masters, Spiritual Entities, we do not know and indeed whose existence we resolutely deny.

The Masters use methods which our science does not recognize (mental connecting), sometimes they tell us things that are so far from our normal way of thinking as to appear inconceivable.

I cannot rationally demonstrate that these "methods" are correct.

The only thing I can say in defence of this way of thinking, that my mind sometimes struggles to understand, is that I trust that the voice I hear is the one of a truth which is higher than the one I can see from here, from matter.

And to You, dear readers, I ask you to do the same if you want to find the great treasure that I have discovered here.

*"... giving mankind
intuition as a
tool of true
knowledge"*

Prologue.

February 4th 2010.

I am beginning this new book.

I do not know what the topic will be, I only know that I have to restart to write something.

Strange, isn't it?

I would never have thought that I could begin to write a book under this premise.

The Masters have suggested that I re-read the notes I took from a course that I followed in 2006 : - " The Invisible Masters" by Igor Sibaldi [32].

I begin to leaf through them and I ask myself where I should stop.

Some specific notes are highlighted to me and I summarize and change them according to the signs which come to me along the way.

The Masters tell me that I have to connect to them in a specific way and they point out a detailed method of doing so. It is not generalizable, it only regards me.

The way to connect with the Masters.

The garden.

The first thing I have to do is to arrange a meeting place in advance.

I have to look for a place in my "mind" where I am able to meet the Masters. An appropriate place could be a garden, somewhere open and natural. The priority is to identify the general "geometry" in such a way as to allow me to move. In order to make the garden more "mine" and more identifiable with my "mind" it has to be "furnished" in some way.

I can place objects of different types in the garden, both natural and "artificial". It is better if the objects are already known to me, it makes it easier to visualize it.

I can bring anything I want into the garden: furniture, my computer, a waterfall, a couch or even a mountain, there is no problem with space and even less with transport!

It is better not to put animated beings in for the moment.

The furnishing of the garden is a symbolic representation of the "furnishing" of my life.

The Masters, as we shall see, will give me advice on the furnishing, and if the case may be, they will tell to throw out something old and replace it with something new.

I will only be able to change one part, the obvious meaning being that not all of my life is to be thrown away.

A request to completely change the furniture has the obvious meaning that "my life has taken the wrong direction".

How to get into the garden.

I will use methods borrowed from the shamanic culture to get into the garden, I have already used them with notable success in the past.

I have to get myself into a comfortable position, seated with my back straight. I will use the same position as I used to when I meditated[1], kneeling down on a rug and seated on an old cushion.

It is a comfortable position which easily allows the back to be kept straight for a long time. The comfort of the position has always been something which betters my concentration, I have never been able to meditate in the Oriental style, sitting on the floor with my legs crossed, after a while I would lose my balance and would have to get up to avoid becoming stiff.

It is better if I stay in the dark or with little light, preferably in a silent setting.

I relax, as I know how for a couple of minutes, then I begin with a small "imaginative" voyage where I find myself in a very bright tunnel with a very cosy white light.

At the end of the tunnel the light becomes brighter, walking slowly, I go towards it. To get there takes a little more than 20 seconds.

When I get there I feel completely wrapped in this really intense light, I stay there briefly for a couple of seconds.

Then I go immediately to my garden. I walk around a little and if I feel like it, I will get to a piece of furniture which I will find at the next entrance. After looking around, I set my self up in an especially calm and comfortable spot, sitting or lying down, whatever pleases me most.

The Master arrives.

At this point I ask the Master to meet me. He will emerge from somewhere, always the same, from behind a tree for example, and will come towards me, I will sit close and we can begin our conversation.

---

1   I meditated for a few years in a row until 2007 when I met the Masters who advised me to interrupt that practice and to concentrate on material action.

The use of verification.

In order to be completely sure that I am actually speaking with Him, I can ask Him for verification.

This verification can refer to the fact that He is really "my" Master or to any affirmation that He gives me.

When I ask for verification He answers by identifying a specific point in a book used for reference, e.g. a passage from the Bible.

It is not strictly necessary that the Bible is the book used, it could be any text. It is only necessary to establish the text to be used at the beginning and keep to that as the reference.

If the Bible is used, His answer will indicate if it is the Old or New Testament, the page, the column and the number of the line, notes and chapter titles are excluded.

At this point all I have to do is simply remember what He tells me.

When I leave the garden I go and single out the point shown me by the Master and I can check if the written text answers the question I asked Him or not.

This possibility of "verification" is used as an aid and stimulates subsequent conversations with the Masters. It is a type of reassurance on the goodness of the connection.

The conversation with the Master.

Going back to the conversation with the Master, He points me towards the topics that are necessary to discuss. It is not my place to ask questions, He talks to me and I will remember everything He says.

I have to pay careful attention to the messages I receive and as soon as I leave the garden I write them down, if not, I will forget them.

Before going to meet the Master I have to imagine Him in a form. I can give Him the semblance of an "imaginary" person, not anyone I know, it could be a "historical" figure or someone dressed in a certain way or an unknown specific face.

Giving a form to the Master is important because his presence is detached from any specific location (He is everywhere), and otherwise he would miss my contact.

The Master will speak to me about my conscious wishes, every wish is a type of possibility which gives a hypothesis of what could happen to me even, if you like, a temptation to act upon. In any case, a wish is never seen as a possible sin, (there are no hidden moral judgements) it is always seen as a possibility of mine. The Masters will always be clear on whether my wishes are appropriate or not and explain why.

They also clarify my most unpleasant and darkest desires, these are the ones which are the most important to explain. I have to understand why they are not desires (possibilities) to follow and what to do now that they are no longer my desires.

All this serves to help me concentrate on my most luminous wishes or moreover, on the possibilities for my growth.

In order to identify my darkest desires, I have to face up to my most hidden part, my ugliest, most arid and infertile "landscape". It is here that I will find my interior "dragon", the one I have to defeat.

The Master is the Ally who helps me defeat the dragon, a symbol[2] that has a precise meaning: *"the past which does not want to be passed"*. The dragon needs nutrition in order to stay alive, I am part of its nutrient, as long as the dragon is alive it will drain a part of my energy and leave me without enough strength to move to the future, or better still the next level of my growth.

I can only get there following "luminous" desires.

Therefore, I have to kill the dragon.

The conclusion of the meeting.

At a certain point, the Master tells me the meeting is over. After thanking Him, I make my way back to the luminous "ball" of the tunnel, enter quickly and go back to the room I left from.

I turn on the light and immediately get a hold of a notebook and write down everything the Master told me.

---

2   Symbol means the conduit which connects us to a determined "truth".

Why do I use this method?

I do not understand why the Masters showed me the above means of connecting.

It is a mixture of techniques that I used in the past and that I have not used for some time.

By connecting me to the story of the dragon makes me think that want me to complete an unfinished task.

Obviously there is something old that they want me to shake off. Something that the Masters told me at the beginning of my third book [4] comes to mind *"I still have free myself from some excess of mental ties that my little head continues to produce"*.

The moment has arrived to cleanse myself, but of what?

The Voyage.

Two days after the communication that I spoke about, I finally find the time and peace to apply the "connection" that was shown to me.

I say "voyage" synthetically to describe the method that was shown me as a reminder of the "shamanic voyages" which I took in the past and which offer numerous analogies.

I remember with pleasure the shamanic voyage, it was probably among the strangest techniques that I have experimented with and it taught me how to contact and actually "feel" spiritual entities which circle around us, but moreover, this technique almost always gave good results also in relation to subsequent feedback at a material level.

Therefore I face the voyage with trust.

In the rush of getting ready, I forgot the suggestion to put a form to the Master, but it did not create serious problems.

The room is almost completely dark, a solitary candlelight helps me relax, soon after I enter the tunnel and feel at ease and I begin to walk slowly, the ball of light at the end stuns me for a moment and in a fraction of a second I am in my "garden".

It is more than a garden, it is an enormous green meadow.

I furnish it a little, I create a small hill, rigorously green, that grows under my feet. I put a two-seater wooden bench at the top, its long side parallel to the line which connects the centre of the hill to the large meadow in front.

The bench is not exactly in the centre of the hill but slightly to one side, facing centre. I turn my head to the left and overlook the meadow, it seems a bit naked. I hurry to furnish it some more with two rows of high trees

6

that part from either side of the hill and meet up on the horizon, a large upturned V, a perspective V.

Their positioning seems to suggest the vastness and enormity of everything around me. Somewhere on the horizon they should meet at a certain point.

Is this an analogy for life?

This " garden" is not bad.

Something is missing though, on the side opposite the large meadow. I put the slopes of a rather steep mountain in place, there is a vertical fissure through which there is a slightly sinuous path that allows access to an internal, vertical cylinder like aperture, here there is a magnificent waterfall surrounded by the walls of the mountain, which partially forms a small lake at the bottom.

Beautiful!

I do not think I need anything else.

I call the Master.

Oh! ... I forgot to give him a "form".

The first thing that comes to mind is the Druid from Asterix, a wise old man with a long white robe, long hair and beard. Sounds right.

Where should I make him appear from?

From the waterfall!

A shape that appears gradually.

I see him coming down from inside the mountain, out of the fissure and along from behind the side of the hill.

The image of the Druid does not seem too convincing, it is too cartoon-like. I decide to give it a more human form, I think of the famous self-portrait of Leonardo da Vinci[3].

Now the "vision" is more believable and my mind is more satisfied.

The Master comes closer and sits on the bench beside me. He begins to talk to me straight away, giving me the "verification" of his identity as requested.

He tells me to read the Old Testament from the Bible [1], page 25, second column, 13th line from the bottom.

---

3   "Head of a man with Beard" (the so-called self-portrait) attributed to Leonardo and currently held in the Biblioteca Reale of Turin.

Then He tells me that this meeting is about putting certain things right inside me in order to free myself once and for all of past baggage.

I have still got partial residues of pride that I must get rid of. I remember that pride is a "horrible beast" according to the Masters.

In the first of my books [2], They told me to distinguish the dark side from the bright side of pride,

> *"pride defends your defects and throws you to the perils*
> *of danger; in fact it is the source of evil."*

For example, I sometimes notice that I find myself daydreaming about my meetings with famous personalities or on the fame I could have with the spread of these writings. These considerations are games in my head which keep me attached to a residue of pride that takes form in the specific desire of affirmation that my personality[4] manifests.

It is a dark desire that will have to be eliminated; a dragon to kill.

It should be clear that I am not saying that I cannot meet those personalities or that I cannot be famous through the diffusion of these writings, but this must come about without the proud desire of affirmation of my personality.

To overcome this obstacle I have to consciously block out the stream of thoughts that lead me to the above, when I notice their appearance.

All things considered, it is quite simple, when I think "bad" thoughts, I have to change what I am thinking.

I wonder if it is easy as I say …?

If I can free myself from this residual obstacle, things should go well and I should be able to fulfil what is predicted of me (to follow my destiny with all my available strength).

The Master says that meetings like today are not strictly necessary and if we have to meet, I can do it through the usual way as outlined in my third book [4].

After telling me where I am going wrong, He cheers me up by adding that I am still his "pupil" and that I will achieve what I have to, it is just that I will have to work on it more.

---

4   N.B. Here we talk about personality not soul.

He also tells me that is enough for today and if He tells me more I will forget it and therefore it will be of no use. Feeling his affection fills me with joy and I thank Him. He returns as He came, fading into the waterfall.

I leave as well and go back to my room as He had indicated. Turning on the light, I start to write down everything He had told me in pencil.

I feel serene.

The verification.

I had asked the Master for a verification of His identity in the voyage I have just described.

I was told to find a certain line in a certain page of the bible.

I immediately looked it up, Genesis: V.

"Methuselah lived to be nine hundred and sixty-nine".

What should I make of it?

"Are you really my Master?" I asked him, the answer came back "Methuselah lived to be nine hundred and sixty-nine".

Given that the answer referred to someone who lived to be almost a thousand years old made me think that the Master wanted to answer "yes, I am really a special person".

The fact that this person was Methuselah, already well known in the Bible and by tradition to be an exemplar of long life, led me to believe that the Master is someone who goes beyond time usually reserved for human beings.

The word " lived" led me to believe that I found myself in the company of a living being, even if not of a physical life.

Basically, I came to the conclusion that what was in front of me was a special living entity which goes beyond time.

This was enough to convince me that I was with a spiritual Master.

The fact that He was asked if He was "my" Master and He did not give a specific reply is clear enough; the Master could not be "mine" and therefore could not answer yes.

My question was partially correct and the answer I got pertained only to the correct part.

Not bad for a verification, is it?

And now what do I do?

I have clearly understood that I have to modify my excess of pride.

What should the argument be in the book I am writing?

I certainly have not understood yet!

I ask the Masters to give me the right prompt, a clue by means of another "verification", similar to the one just analyzed which had a great success.

I ask them to tell me where I can go to "read" the theme for this new book without having to take another voyage.

They tell me to go to the Old Testament again, page 201, 2nd column, 7th line from the bottom. I take the Bible and read the 7th line from the bottom:

"… here is all of the territory. Well then, you are able to come back here".

Let's see if we can understand something.

I ask if the answer is about territory and I am immediately told no.

The sense of the discussion lies in "Well then, you are able to come back here".

Re-reading the phrase carefully, it becomes immediately clear: the Masters want me to say "by doing something specific, I will have the possibility of returning to the true knowledge of the Masters".

This entire book will focus on the true knowledge of the Masters and on my possibility of re-entering into it.

It is a really beautiful theme.

Masters, You have, as always, an extraordinary ability to enthuse me. Thanks.

A continuous miracle.

I do not know why the answer of the Masters enthused me so much at the end of the previous chapter, They simply re-iterated things that They have been trying to tell me in different ways, over the last couple of years.

And I still felt enthusiastic.

A thought comes into my head that this enthusiasm could be due to the way in which the message was communicated to me. The "verification" and its subsequent interpretation were almost like a lightening bolt of intuition in my mind.

In fact, thinking about it with our habitual mental canons makes it seem really strange.

How could it be that a "little voice" in my head could point me to a specific line in a dense book?

How could my rational mind reach the logical enough conclusion that the argument written is the same one which I had been following for the last two years?

The probability that this could happen by chance, I would say is rather low, if not zero.

And yet it happened.

But what is it?

Is it magic?

Is it a miracle?

Or simply a mysterious event?

It seems clear to me.

I got enthused because I had assisted at the happening of a mysterious event which left me pleasantly surprised.

We can also call it a "miracle", a little miracle, so we can fire up our imagination and enthusiasm even more.

These miracles are happening to me one after the other, in fact, I could say that I am in a state of "continuous miracle". Obviously, the fact I am still enthusiastic means that I am still not used to this, it is beautiful from an emotional point of view, but maybe it only means our brain is not used to, and cannot get used to any unexpected "happening" that occurs outside of our physical world.

But what is the substance of this miracle?

Putting it simply, it is a strange phenomenon we do not recognize and cannot explain how it happened. It is something that goes beyond our mental parameters and habits, I mean habits in relation to our physical world.

By analyzing the situation more carefully, we immediately see that even our physical world is permeated by an infinite quantity of continuous miracles which we become used to and are therefore considered normal.

We do not know anything about the origins of these events or how they work, but by seeing them every day and being assured by our science of their factual occurrence, they become real and normal.

For example, it is considered normal that DNA exists in our cells, a long, regular helix that holds all our information, scientists[5] assure us of its existence and they can perceive its functioning mechanism, and yet, we are forced to consider it as a true miracle without thinking about what it can do or how it originated.

Another example which is so often discounted as to be not even taken into consideration, is the existence of the Earth and within it an environment that allows the growth of humankind.

The probability that so many factors could combine to produce something so suitable to human life is so small that it is almost zero.

We do not know how to explain how it happened.

Is that not a miracle?

---

5   Of course you know that the discovery of DNA is due to the Nobel Prize winners Watson and Crick. However, maybe you do not know that the discovery of its helical shape, seen by everyone as one of the most important results of human mental rationality, was made by Crick under the effects of LSD, in a state which no one would dare call rational [16].

We could go on and make a never-ending list of miracles or of strange and inexplicable phenomena which happen on a daily basis and rarely leave us surprised or amazed.

Magic, miracle, mystery ...

Have you ever asked yourselves why these inexplicable things happen? Why do they continually unfold before our very eyes, before the eyes of men who think they know everything or who delude themselves into thinking that they could know everything? Behind everything that is mysterious or unintelligible there is some kind of sense.

Maybe, if we try hard, we will manage to understand something.

A course in miracles.

I would say that the Masters are giving me real "course in miracles".

By way of keeping to the theme, they invite me to read a book, aptly called "A course in miracles"[6] [31].

According to this book[7] *a miracle can be expressed in various mental or physical forms, it has one essential characteristic, it is a sudden freedom from perceived errors.*

A miracle simply consists of the removal of anything which impedes knowledge of the presence of love.

When this moment is verified, let's call it the "sacred instant", we feel God's peace and subsequently we can see things as they really are and not through the clouds of our own self-arrogance or ignorance.

---

6   The book is considered a milestone in terms of modern spiritual texts. It is channelled between dreams and mental suggestion. It was written by an atheist psychologist, Helen Schucman and her head of department William Tethord, of the Columbia-Presbyterian Medical Centre of New York. It is a thick tome with more than 1200 pages. The cover is characteristically blue with gold letters and is sub-divided into exercises for students and a manual for teachers. It has sold more than a million copies and has created self-managed study groups all over the world [7].

7   A large part of the text in italics are extracts of a synopsis of the book cited in [7]. They have been partially modified or cited in an adequate form to satisfy the requests of the Masters to present what, in their opinion, corresponds to "true knowledge".

I would say that up to this point, we are in complete symphony with everything the Masters have taught me.

But let's go further.

The book makes an important *distinction between reality and non-reality, or more so between knowledge and perception. Reality/knowledge is beyond time, "it might not be recognized, but it cannot be changed"*.

On the other hand, non-reality/perception, is the world which we normally perceive, which involves an interpretation of the facts; that is what we perceive appears real but it is so only through the lenses with which we see it. However, what is real is not perceived but is known, it is unequivocal and therefore, reliable.

In the book we also find another important *distinction between "special" relationships and "sacred relationships".*

The first consist of desires of the ego and many people only have this type of relationship. This type of relationship is a way of excluding God from one's own life.

On the other hand, the second type, the "sacred relationships", allow the intervention of God and are the transformation of the old special relationships.

When we ask God, or more specifically the Holy Ghost, to enter into our relationships, changes are quickly verified and "suddenly His objective takes the place of yours".

In a special relationship, *it is the objective on which it is built that gives it sense, if we do not obtain what we want from it we tend to break the relationship, after that the emphasis is placed what we do not want,* or more so, on what the ego wants.

The problem is that we are destined to always feel insecure in our relationships because they are not built on solid foundations.

We believe that we know what is best for us, but in fact our ego really does not have an objective for our relationship except but to use it for our benefit.

God, on the other hand, has a well-defined objective for relationships and therefore we have faith in the fact that this objective will come to be revealed.

At the beginning you need *faith to feel the presence of the Holy Ghost after a short while this is transformed into conviction.*

This gives us the chance to *save our relationships from ourselves,* or to transform our special relationships into sacred relationships, or to enter into relationships with a real objective: divine.

The book highlights the *necessity of forgiving because it singles out forgiveness as a means of liberating us from mistaken perceptions and of seeing the truth again.*

"Forgiveness is the means through which we will remember. Through forgiveness the way of thinking of the world is overturned".

Forgiving, means seeing the essential innocence of a person, the truth behind the façade. When we are able to do so, instead of continuously feeling the need to judge and attack, we will have a healthy relationship.

We rediscover in the *"Course in Miracles"* that *"the only thing that is real is love,"* with the logical consequence that everything else is an illusion.

By praying and meditating it is possible to rectify our mistaken perceptions regarding this reality and when we see a mistaken perception, it will not be our ego which allows us to see the light but only the understanding of the true reality beyond the ego.

If we try to solve our problems only through thought, the only effect that we obtain is that the questions and answers remain connected to the ego.

An "honest" question instead, is one in which we "ask something that we do not know".

A "true" answer will be true today as it will be tomorrow, it is reached in a sacred moment, in a momentary flash of awareness, it is a gift from God.

When we experience this truth, it seems like a miracle. It has not come from us as we currently know ourselves but from that part of us that has always been uniquely with God.

Our separation from God is illusory.

To get this type of guide we have to forget thought and simply be still.

"All things find answers in peace and quiet and all problems are resolved in tranquillity".

Well then, who should be in control?

The ego or something else?

When we are confused about who or what we are, it means that we are struggling between what our ego desires and that which is naturally ours.

The ego loves being busy in the creation and maintenance of our problems, something which should show us that these problems might not be as real as they appear, but instead are created by a part of us that wants to keep them.

In the book, it is explicitly stated that the *conviction of being a lone entity that hovers around the world is the "deepest madness", because in reality we are at one with God who created us and we always have been.*

Remember what "reconcile yourself" means; when we admit that, *there is no room for doubt or insecurity.*

The *"course"* states that *"all things collaborate for the good. There are no exceptions apart from the judgement which comes from the ego".*

Many people *do not like to talk about God or spiritual questions because every recognition of God shows the "inexistence of the ego itself", and many people identify themselves by their ego.*

Given that the ego believes in itself as an entity created by itself means that *it cannot accept the totality of God.*

What does the second[8] coming of God mean?

Not the physical arrival of a Christ like figure on Earth but rather the end of the dominion of the ego.

The Holy Ghost is God's messenger, he is sent to cure the tormented misunderstandings that the ego has made appear as real.

The book "a course in miracles" is a miracle in itself.

It was communicated to its authors through channelling, or more so with the same mode as the origins of all religions on Earth.

It *mainly teaches, as do all the religions on Earth, that separation is an illusion and that a renewed awareness of our unity with God makes everything possible, every miracle.*

A miracle becomes "normality" when we are in line with a superior power, my connection to the Masters is nothing more than a continuous miracle which is becoming normality.

---

8   The Masters tell me here that God the creator has already acted directly on Earth, not once, but ten times and not all of them on mankind; the above action will become the eleventh and will correspond to an evolutive leap (some say "quantum leap") this will constitute the real basis of all the talk about 2012. This evolutive leap is what other writers have defined as the attainment of the "Christ dimension" [22,23], in other words, the reaching of a state in which it is normal to feel united with the Creator.

Human knowledge.

Reason, the instrument of human knowledge.

We all know what reason is, the ability to think, discern and determine logical relationships and make judgements.

It is peculiarly human.

Renè Descartes, a master of reason, famous for the Cartesian "I think, therefore, I am", said that reason is innate and identifiable in all humans, the problem is that not everyone knows how to use it correctly.

He stated that if used correctly, and he gave us the method to do so [10], we could *"increase our knowledge by degree and progressively reach a maximum point"*.

According to him, this "maximum point" *"would carry our nature to its highest degree of perfection"*.

Great faith in reason.

For we humans, it is obvious to have faith in reason, we are perfectly aware that it is the instrument which allows us to analyze and understand the world around us.

Reason helps our physical survival, to realize projects, to work and to earn a living.

Anyone who has weak "reason" does not have success and at times is taken for an idiot.

Everyone wants to be able to reason well ... obviously!

Reason, superset with logical ability, is often considered synonymous with the mind and is fundamental to live on Earth. As humans, we feel superior to animals whose minds are less developed than ours or who maybe do not have a mind.

We are convinced that our mind is our strength and the instrument through which we can reach, as Descartes said, any type of awareness … and according to some it could even render us omnipotent.

This is only an illusion.

Reason is simply a magnificent tool which allows us to know only what a human being can know, it is the instrument of human knowledge.

The scope of the use of reason.

Reason is a tool which is particularly adapted for the understanding of the mechanisms that develop in the world of matter.

To that end, it has developed a method, "the scientific method", this is an extremely reasonable and efficient way of guaranteeing a exact interpretation of phenomena that happen in the Earth's environment and that limited amount of the Universe seen by us.

This is its great limitation.

It can only interpret the mechanisms of the physical world, indeed only some of these (at least for the moment…).

Human knowledge is therefore directly dependent on reason, this goes well to understand only a part of creation, the part which substantially belongs to the physical dimension.

The interpretation of physical mechanisms is often incomplete. In reality, mankind, because of our way of reasoning, is forced to make a synthesis of the problems analyzed with a restricted way of seeing things as they really are.

The limits of human knowledge.

The need of synthesis is already a great limit and not only that. Let us imagine at least for a moment, that creation is much vaster than only the physical world, what I have already called the "physical dimension", and let us suppose that other impalpable, ethereal and non-physical dimensions exist[9]. Automatically this would render the physical dimension as a subset of something much vaster[10].

It follows as a logical consequence that reason, being suitable to work on the physical dimension, can only reasonably explain a small subset of creation.

Reason would therefore come out as an insufficient instrument to explain creation that goes beyond the physical aspect.

I am certainly not the first to say so.

A phrase of Pascal [29] has stuck with me for a good part of my life. He said:

> "The supreme step of reason lies in the knowledge
> that there is an infinity of things beyond it.
> It is very weak if it fails to acknowledge this."

Knowledge or ignorance?

The Masters are even more decisive in highlighting the limits of human knowledge.

They told me in the past during the interpretation of physical phenomena related to crop circles [3], that human interpretation is not often correct and goes in the wrong direction.

The Master even went on to tell me that He would have to transmit some information to me because He feared that the interpretation of some facts could be "trusted" to human circles who were not up to the task.

The Masters negate the "narrow-minded way of seeing things" which humans have. They also say that human knowledge is "blind" and incapable of seeing what is truly significant and important. It is seen by them as a partial knowledge and therefore so often mistaken that they consider it to be ignorance.

---

9   Even scientists who only use reason are convinced that the only way to arrive at a rational explanation that is at least a little congruent with the universe is to introduce other dimensions which are linked to and complementary with the physical.

10 Believe me it is much, much, much vaster.

The Masters have no doubt that we are talking about ignorance, and their intervention must unmask it as such.

The help they are giving has this end.

They told me:

"We deem that we have met you to create a list of discoveries
from which the disappearance of ignorance will give us
the guarantee of the subsequent step forward.
Give ignorance its name."

The Masters wanted to tell me that the meetings I had with A and B were at their request to allow us to make discoveries, in fact, a series of discoveries, whose final aim would be the gradual disappearance of ignorance in the specific field already discussed.

Knowledge (the disappearance of ignorance), in that single argument, or part of it, allows us to face up to a further step of awareness.

Now I expect to "go it alone", without the help of A or B.

My task is to go forward and *"give to ignorance its name"*, to unveil false conviction and knowledge and recognize them for the ignorance and mistaken awareness that they are.

Beware of reason.

They put me on my guard and warmly advised me to be wary of reason.

They told me that I could reach a different and superior knowledge by being "suspicious" of current knowledge and to forget about the present and its given wisdom.

Human beings behave in relation to their knowledge, looking around at current behaviour it is easy to see that there is the clear sensation that something does not quite square up.

They told me:

"Human behaviour brings pain to the planet".

This led me to understand that human beings are making the planet uninhabitable not only from an environmental and physical point of view but also from an ideological one.

This "mental"[11] pollution has its effects on other humans and also on the "non-human" population that share this planet.

This behaviour of polluting plays a fundamental role in the way that a type of human pride makes mankind see itself as self-sufficient and the main object of creation.

Human beings have managed to transform heavenly messages, meant to help and correctly guide them, into a type of pride in having a "Great God" to whom they erects temples and set themselves in opposition to the God of others.

This is the way things will have to go, by that I mean that we should mistrust current knowledge and introduce a different one.

The origins of great human discoveries.

One of the reasons that humans base their faith in reason is in the admiration of the great results that knowledge has brought about during the course of history and which has surged ahead in the last centuries characterized by scientific culture.

In reality, we humans have made important discoveries which have eased and improved our existence by no mean amount. But are we really sure that these discoveries can be based on our reason alone?

We exaggerate our admiration for those people who, thanks to some amazing discovery, are defined as geniuses.

Their genius is attributed to an uncommon intelligence.

We identify this intellectual insight with well functioning reason.

But it is not like this.

If things were like this, we would never be able to arrive at effective new knowledge.

Reason, as we normally see it, is like a computer in which known input is analysed by up to date software which, on the basis of known algorithms

---

11 Defining exactly what "mental" is, is not easy. We could simply define it as a "series of thoughts which result from an energetic capacity capable of provoking or impeding change". It has the ability to connect itself with the "mental" of other beings and give rise to even more powerful and active energies.

of calculus, produces output which seems "new", but in fact, is only an elaboration of things we already know.

Therefore, it is not a new discovery, it is only a closer examination of something we already know.

A computer cannot do more and neither can reason, or at least our idea of it.

During the course of history, discoveries have come about which have strongly negated this re-elaboration of known data. Some geniuses have gone "off the rails" of already acquired knowledge and have effectively introduced new paradigms of understanding.

They have made a real leap forward in something that was unknown in terms of human knowledge, detached from everything that had been known before.

We often need to make an irrational and illogical leap.

New awareness cannot be supported by our reason or at least our idea of reason.

This would be a good point to open a window on the most important discoveries of the past and to try and understand why people like Leonardo da Vinci were able to introduce radical new aspects of understanding.

My answer is simple, these geniuses had access to a fount of knowledge external to humans.

The example of Crick in the discovery of the DNA helix is very significant and has been cited before.

In my opinion, it is an example which well illustrates the development of an advanced cognitive event.

An already notable knowledge of the argument is required as a basis, by the researcher.

At this point the talented researcher must possess the ability to read the suggestions that come from the outside.

In Crick's case this suggestion was the vision of a helix while the drug had taken him into a dimension which we normally define as hallucinatory and without sense.

In itself, it was a kid's game to associate the shape of the helix with the problem he was working on, but it led to an amazing discovery.

A person without any foundation in the subject would have made nothing of the helix, indeed, it would have been seen as a useless but pleasant hallucination.

The drug allowed Crick to enter a dimension normally defined as an "altered state" compared to the normal state of vigil consciousness.

Drugs[12] produce this effect as is well known in the shamanic culture[13] which, among other things, has produced safer and less degenerative techniques to access these non physical "worlds".

Huxley [17] was aware of this when he knocked on his "doors of perception" under the influence of mescalin[14].

From these experiments[15] he came to the conclusion that a person in a normal state of consciousness is not capable of perceiving the world as it is, but can only give order to things according to their pre-existent categories and labels.

He stated that, *"our brain and nervous system are a reduction valve which show us a minimal part of the consciousness of a broadened mind"*.

He also said that language *"is simply a way in which we codify these reduced perceptions. In its favour, it allows us to access and know accumulated experience, however it crystallizes fixed ways of seeing the world."*

Furthermore, *"our language and our way of perceiving reality are moulded by our need to survive and thus we only admit a limited reality. The need to transcend the normal sense of self is also part of human nature."*

---

12 The psychotropic effects of the drug reduce the normal perceptive mechanisms by also chemically intervening on our physical body. But the main effect is of an "energetic" type, increasing the perception of our subtle bodies of the lower level (etheric, astral and mental) and at the same time reducing our perception of our physical body.

13 In my first book [2] I partially dealt with some aspects of shamanic culture, which I studied closely for more than five years. Now the Masters make me understand the serious limitations of this discipline, even although it is a real opening into non-physical worlds.

14 Mescalin is an extract from the root of peyote, a Mexican cactus, which since time immemorial has been used by the local population thanks to its introspective hallucinatory properties.

15 A similar experiment was recently carried out by Graham Hancock with the aim of demonstrating that the introduction of graphic images in human history (through cave paintings etc.) could have been done under the influence of psychotropic plants and altered states derived from them.

The drug takes us to a wider reality than the one we are used to.

I am far from suggesting that we should use drugs to experiment with these worlds.

Indeed I would say it is better to avoid them because of the known psycho-physical degenerative problems that they cause.

The Masters clearly highlighted that our real growth comes through maintaining control of ourselves.

By giving to our inner self more.

Relying on drugs, means a dependency on something external and thus giving ourselves less.

"*We lose part of our self-control and we live a life that is more autonomous (detached) and sad.*"

Drugs are not the ideal means to access superior knowledge. These worlds can also be reached through normal anaesthesia but there is only a little difference between this and drug use I have already described.

These worlds can be reached through numerous techniques of "profound contemplation" of shamanic origin.

Sometimes these are similar to modern hypnosis.

The initial paragraphs of this book speak in detail about the experience of one of my "trips" of this kind, as you can see it allowed me to go beyond the rigid confines of the mind and acquire "knowledge" that normal reasoning is incapable of identifying.

It is possible to enter deeper dimensions even while sleeping.

Intuition.

I maintain that the entry into an enormous "knowledge tank" of wider understanding by those geniuses and artists who have introduced the greatest innovations in history has been done so by using what we would normally call "intuition".

Yes, that is right.

That banal and simple intuition which many of us know we have but we often do not know what it is. Some call it the "sixth sense" while others relegate it to a simple "instinct".

Often it is that sudden idea which solves a problem that has bugged us for ages while we are thinking about something completely different or it could be that strange sensation which warns us of imminent danger and maybe saves our life.

My initiation.

Talking about intuition, do you know how I first clearly noticed the existence of these external "suggestions" which triggered off a long activity of internal searching, the fruit of which is also this book?

Let me tell you the story of my "initiation".

I was on my honeymoon near Mont Blanc in Val d'Aosta.

My wife and I had been passionate about the mountains for years, so much so that we wanted to enjoy the exertions of the heights as well as the other type of "exertions" required on honeymoon …

An old friend, a long-time expert of glaciers and snow, accompanied us on a trip on the glacier of Estellette at the bottom of Val Veny.

During this trip we found ourselves at the face of a glacier where we saw the remains of an airplane which had crashed some years before. I have kept a part of the bodywork as a souvenir and it should still be around somewhere.

At a certain height, just above 2,500 metres, our friend stopped. His advancing years didn't allow him to climb too high. Maddalena and I carried on by ourselves along a steep and narrow snowfield surrounded by sheer walls.

We wanted to reach a saddle from where you could enjoy a fantastic view of the Lex Blanche glacier below.

I hadn't seen such a spectacle of crevices and seracs before or since.

Leaving Maddalena there, I went on alone to try and find a refuge, which according to the maps, should have been nearby. The path was complete rock so I didn't bother to take crampons or an ice pick, unburdening myself of this weight I figured that I would be much quicker and only have to "abandon" my better half for a few minutes.

At a certain point a herd of peaceful ibexes crossed my path, I found out later that this was a rare occurrence in these parts. Immediately beyond I came upon a steep snowfield only a few metres wide which I easily crossed thanks to the good consistency of the snow which was neither too soft nor too icy.

I carried on a little further without managing to see the refuge and I decided to go back so as to curtail my journey.

And here comes the good part.

Some metres before the snowfield, I heard a voice in my head, it was strong and clear, " STOP!"

I stopped, alarmed.

"You are about to fall on the snowfield. When you fall remember to do a double sideways roll to your left and cling on to the rock mass you will find immediately below."

My brain immediately forgot the state of alarm and the strange if not absurd advice ... maybe it was a hallucination due to the height.

I got closer to the snowfield and I began to cross it with the same confidence as before, I already knew the snow and knew that it was safe.

Halfway across the snowfield and as if by an unbelievable trick of nature, the snow, which had been compact before, had transformed into ice.

Anyone who has slipped on a snowfield, even if it's not too steep, knows fine well how difficult, if not impossible it is to stop without the aid of an ice pick.

And I had nothing.

My brain remembered the advice given to me some metres before and I began to roll over sideways to my left enough to move transversally and cling on to the rock mass below.

A completely unnatural movement.

I got up and sat on a rock, a few metres from the ibexes who lazily observed me as nothing more than an annoying but harmless intrusion.

I trembled like only a few times before in my life with such a rush of adrenalin that even seated, I felt as though I was jumping on the rock.

I remained still for a few minutes while an avalanche of thoughts crazily went through my brain.

I thought about the slope with the steep snowfield which ended nesting on a vertical rocky wall, if I had finished down there, I would have fallen hundreds of metres.

"How did I manage to risk my life, just married, with my young wife waiting a few metres below for me?"

"It would have been absurd to die like this now!"

"How did I save myself?"

"And that incredible voice that saved me?"

"And that absurd movement! ..."

Slowly but surely, my thoughts started to calm down and I reached Maddalena, thinking that it was a miracle to see her again.

Since then, I have thought about that escapade hundreds of times and every time, I always feel a debt of immense gratitude to that voice which saved my life.

Many years later I got to know who spoke it, but maybe I will tell you about that another time.

For the moment it is enough to know that for an instant, I was connected to a higher form of knowledge which warned me of the imminent danger and told me how to escape it, a miraculous stroke of intuition.

Intuition!

Our reason does not know what it is ... it is something normal!

I have told the story of how I was saved from falling to a lot of people, most of them say that I had simply been helped by my instinct and experience of the mountains.

That is it, normal!

No!

It was another miracle like the ones we spoke about previously, even if almost everyone considers it to have been a normal event.

They do not perceive the characteristics of the extraordinary event which, in fact, it was.

From that initiation I began to better understand the strength of intuition and gradually, what is behind it.

Intuition is a tool which allows us to reach a less limited knowledge than that authorized by our reason.

But, exactly what is this intuition?

If you can be patient, I will tell you some more.

The sense of mystery.

From what I have told you up to now it appears clear that I believe that an open attitude is fundamental towards something which is not immediately understandable to the mind.

We have to pay careful attention to a mysterious sphere that in many ways is connectable to dreams and often to the creation of myths.

Carl Gustav Jung, a giant of psychology, tried to tackle this subject and the Masters singled him out to me as being reliable in the conclusions he reached in his books from the point of view of true knowledge.

They suggested that I read one of his books called "Memories, dreams and reflections" [18].

Jung's visions, dreams and fantasies are considered by him to be his own *"greatest wealth"* because he retains these elements to be *"the prism through which we can perceive the collective human psyche."*

That book is probably the only one in which Jung speaks of his personal experience of God. He simply sees God *"as the power of the universe with all his light and darkness, his randomness and infiniteness."*

He concludes that *"God actually wants to cause us to have "evil thoughts", that go against current morals so we can go back to him independently."*

He argues that *"a person who is genuinely spiritual must be a free thinker who needs to experience God and not be content with mere faith."*

As you may have already understood, the Masters tell me more or less the same thing.

This idea that *"the divine is not all light and sweetness, and the conviction that Christianity has never been able to face up to the problem of evil in a satisfactory manner"* [7], made him have a problematic relationship with mainstream Christianity.

However, what is closer to the heart of the matter is his conviction that *"everyone has religious ideas in themselves, hints of infinity and deeper meaning."*

Those who repress these aspects of themselves, develop neurosis.

These people *"would never be split against themselves if they had lived in an earlier epoch in which their life would have been more rigidly woven in myth, ritual and nature.*

Modern man is too objective and his spiritual horizons too restricted: many live exclusively on the plain of the conscious and rational mind.

Only by filling the abyss between their ego and the unconscious mind, will they be able to return to a state of complete mental health."

Therefore we can only be sane by integrating the "mystery" in ourselves.

The spiritual dimension was a fundamental psychological element for Jung.

All the work I am doing with Masters and other personal experiences make me fully aware of the truth of his statements. When the question is posed *"Do you believe in God?"*, he answered: *"I don't believe - I know."*

An answer that can only be given if our obscure part is completely integrated in ourselves, if it becomes "experience".

Jung distinguished between two personalities within an individual: *"personality 1, is that which we consider "I", and personality 2, is that which we consider "the other"."*

The "other" represents that part of us endowed with a timeless and imperishable wisdom.

In my discussions with the Masters, personality 1 is similarly called "personality" and essentially contains psychological features of the body in which we are incarnated; a temporary body and therefore a temporary personality.

I prefer to call personality 2, "soul". It does not die and it contains all the wisdom we have managed to accumulate in time during the various lives passed on Earth.

Jung dedicated himself to the study of personality 2, "the other", "the shadow", "the true self".

He perfectly realized that *"when we don't manage to integrate "the other" with personality 1, we tend to project things that we don't recognize onto other people or things, often with harmful consequences".*

In substance, this means that if we cannot feel our soul, which gives us completeness, we are forced out of ourselves to seek what we cannot find, the wholeness within ourselves which we lack.

However our soul is something that is unreachable through reason alone.

We need other means of ... investigation.

Jung gave Freud credit *"for identifying our dreams as the most important source of information regarding unconscious processes"* and he praised him *"for giving humanity a tool which had seemed irredeemably lost."*

Jung detached himself from Freud because he did not share his complete belief that "repressed sexuality" was the key to every type of human behaviour and to every type of artistic and spiritual expression of man.

He undertook an independent study arriving at his famous idea of the "*collective unconsciousness*" or better still, "*a widened human mind in which every individual takes part and manifests itself in images, symbols, dreams and myths which make up all cultures*".

Images, symbols, dreams and myths are all expressions of a personal or collective mystery which complete a person or a society.

According to Jung " *the "process of mythologizing" gives an allure to the life of anyone who experiments with it, and once tried, it is difficult to do without.*"

And "*why should we do without?*" he asked.

"*Dreams and the unconscious are of little relevance as far as the rational intellect is concerned, but if they can enrich our emotive life, their value can certainly not be negated. If we live a purely rational existence, privy of complexity, without ever considering our dreams and our fantasies, we become mono-dimensional*".

"*Looking for perfect explanations means we never pause on the incomprehensible, on the mysteries of time and space, and it is the mysterious that gives life sense*".

Here Jung says something that the Masters often referred to. We should point our attention to the unknown.

In fact, we live on Earth because we have to understand (or better re-understand) everything which seems incomprehensible or mysterious, above all with regard to ourselves.

The sense of mystery is clear however, we exist to gradually unveil it and to return to the complete original knowledge of the Creator.

Sending our submarines to explore the sea of unknown knowledge is not a time filler of human curiosity, it is sense in itself of matter, we are here to rediscover what seems hidden to our reason and above all, that which our soul has not experienced yet.

True knowledge.

What is true knowledge?

Intuition introduces us to a strange sphere where we can draw on wider knowledge compared to that which is normally learned.

Compared to the physical world, we access a superset where the vision of things is wider and the higher the level, the wider the vision.

If we reach the "peak of the mountain" our vision can range over all directions.

It is not very clear where intuition will lead us, but wherever it takes us will let us see more and better.

It is the sphere where our Masters "live", spiritual beings, who are often the origin of "suggestions" which intuition then brings to our reason.

The wide view from up there on top naturally brings us to higher knowledge than that of man who is closed in his restricted earthly sphere.

It is not only a higher knowledge.

If the level we accede to is elevated, and our vision of creation is complete, we are in front of the only <u>true</u> knowledge.

True knowledge can only spring out if it has the possibility to see, to feel and to analyze all of the underlying creation, all of the mechanisms it is composed of, all of the energy which passes through it.

The base is then the power to come out of time as we know it, and to go into a wider time, indeed, to go into a sphere which is out of time where the past, the future and the present exist contemporaneously.

True knowledge is only possible if we go beyond space, time and the various dimensions that creation is made up of.

In other words, only by reaching the "peak of the mountain".

No so such place exists you may say.

For sure, even I thought like that.

But I had to think again, now I know through direct experience that such a place exists and that true knowledge, or at least, a wider than human knowledge is possible.

Thanks to the Masters I also know that the gap between true knowledge and human knowledge is often enormous.

I understood the Masters' worry when they told me:

> *"The gap in knowledge between us and mankind obliges us to*
> *pray from time to time that it is not you to define things."*

They hope, in fact, pray, that at times it is not up to men to interpret things, given the little knowledge and foresight that they have.

It is time that we realize that our vision is short and we need to improve it to access true knowledge.

A new point of view.

Before we gain access to true knowledge, above all else, it is necessary that we try to change our concept of life and existence.

To do that, we need a new tool, different from reason which is "in charge" of our limited understanding.

We need to "see" differently as did ancient man[16].

My limited mind, even if I study all the books, accumulating all existing knowledge produced by mankind, does not help me much if I do not have the aid of a new tool.

I need, we need a new vision or Someone who can see for us. Our reason will turn out to be useful to describe with words or images that are more

---

16 In my third book I highlighted some aspects of the foresight that our ancestors had thousands of years ago. Their findings bear witness to this, and our limited vision makes it difficult to interpret them.

or less comprehensible this "new point of view", which cannot be so new if it was known to our forefathers thousands of years ago.

Intuition as a tool of knowledge.

I have already outlined above how intuition is an adequate tool of knowledge.

Some time ago the Masters made me think about some events from the past, for example I remember a discussion about the ancient Egyptians. They have always been a people that fascinated me, they left such a majestic, and by appearance a somewhat useless and megalomaniacal, heritage.

The Masters asked if, in my opinion

"the Egyptians were megalomaniacs or simply free to express themselves?"

"Was it the fact of being free to look at the sky that inspired them, or was it Heaven itself which made them creative?"

"The shape of the pyramid slanting towards the sky, is it done in such a way to help man reach Heaven or to enable a Heavenly message to reach Earth?"

These questions, somewhat anomalous for a normal interpretation of Egyptian culture, managed to communicate that

"observing the sky is a possibility that belongs to man, but we cannot exclude the possibility that it was Heaven itself which inspired the Egyptians to build such an exaggerated pyramid compared to normal earthly needs such as a tomb or a monument."

"Thinking in relation to the pure and simple creativity of man, the construction of a pyramid becomes a matter of great pride for the people who built it, but maybe those men were not particularly able or creative, they were simply submissive to Beings from a much higher level than them who inspired works exactly like the pyramids."

Here we have it! Intuition, inspiration.

They went on to say:

> " *The connection with these Beings from a higher level was a voyage in which*
> *man obtained information and knowledge that was able to help him.*
> *From this point of view, this spiritual experience did not swell man's*
> *pride, it only acted on his mental state and did not cause damage.*
> *The aim of heaven was to help man to act correctly*
> *and not to act in man's place.*
> *Men instead, transformed this help into a type of pride in having*
> *a Great God, seeing the immenseness of their temples."*

The presence of a heaven which intends to help man to act correctly is clear in these few words.

This is not a heaven that substitutes man, but, thanks to the inspiration and true knowledge contained within, induces man to behave in the right way.

But the men of that period misinterpreted the meaning of this help and transformed it into pride.

It seems like a revised correct version, if I can say so, of the story of Adam and Eve from the Bible, only a little less "fairy tale" like. The serpent tempter fascinated Eve, suggesting that by eating the forbidden fruit[17], she and Adam (mankind) would become like God and have universal wisdom.

It is the same thing!

Man, who could have intuited heavenly and therefore true knowledge, was forced by pride to believe he was self-sufficient in his understanding of creation and thus detached himself from the real source of wisdom.

This is why pride is the root of all evil!

This is why, at the beginning of this book, the Masters taught me about the necessity to free myself from the residual traces of pride still present in me.

---

17 Everyone knows that this fruit was an apple ... but where is it written? I have found no traces of apple in the text of the Bible (Genesis III) [1]. According to Jewish tradition (the Talmud) it was a fig, even Michelangelo knew this. He represented the forbidden tree of knowledge as a fig tree in his panel of the *Original Sin and the banishment from Earthly Paradise* in the Sistine Chapel [11].

When I feel that things "add up" in this way, I get enthusiastic.

Thank you Masters for these continuous sparks of knowledge.

But let us get back to the discussion which was interrupted by this illuminating digression.

The Masters went on to tell me:

"Ten or fourteen thousand years ago … . The dates are not important if what is behind them is not known.
Since the reason for heavenly intervention was not to undergo heavy, annoying and exhausting construction work, the divinity put the "Voyage of collective knowledge" aside in order to inspire only a few men and to challenge the preceding local religions with their Gods and to introduce only one God, Ra, the bringer of light, the knowledge of the world".

They wanted to tell me that by scrambling to precisely define the exact dates of the construction of the pyramids, as modern archaeologists are doing, is a sterile exercise in itself if the sense of these constructions and everything behind them is not known. The reason was certainly not to impose heavy construction work on those populations but to make man act on the basis of heavenly knowledge.

But human pride and man's mania for greatness gained the upper hand and heaven was forced to offer its knowledge only to a few chosen men, in the case of Egypt those who introduced the new religion of Ra, the bringer of light and knowledge to the world, and by trying to demolish the myriad of idols built on the basis of pride and certainly not on the suggestion of heaven.

At this point, my intuition suggests a connection to the story of the Israelites when they broke their pact with God (Exodus XXXII).

Also here men no longer knew what to do with the God of Moses who had liberated them from Egypt.

They no longer heard the word or the suggestions of that God (today I would suggest that they did not have the intuition anymore), their pride in being able to go it alone led them build a new divinity by themselves, a banal golden calf.

It is the same thing, human beings detach themselves from true knowledge and Heavenly suggestion and decide to go their own way.

We are in the same condition today.

The Masters went on:

> *"This Heaven must be thanked, these spiritual beings who have*
> *chosen to help the material side (man) by entering linear time*
> *and giving him intuition as a tool of true knowledge.*
> *As long as inspiration comes from Heaven, man is healthy.*
> *By widening his vision which is normally limited to Earthly*
> *materiality, he can become the spokesman of the entire universe*
> *because by supporting his knowledge on Heaven, which*
> *does not remain hidden but manifest and visible."*

They are telling us that we cannot go on like this.

Our limited vision is a sort of disease which impedes us from reaching true knowledge and as a consequence, our behaviour, supported by false knowledge, cannot be turned towards the right direction.

We must be entirely grateful to those heavenly Beings who have chosen to help mankind, looking over us from their timeless state onto our linear time and giving us intuition as a tool of true knowledge.

The Master is one of these beings and He has all of my gratitude.

The universe must not be seen in reductive terms.

Our "classical learning" has a very limited investigative field and the universe it contemplates is only a small subset of what it really is.

The universe does not exist *"only for going on trips"*.

The universe does not exist only as the subject of academic discourse.

Current thinking always reasons in terms of the *"usefulness of the universe for mankind"*, this is limited and wrong.

Who needs a universe only seen in these reductive terms?

This only satisfies the pride of a limited being who deludes himself by thinking it is in his own interests.

But this is really too little!

If this was the sum total of things, what would be the point of creating a structure so infinitely grand like our physical universe?

There would be no "spatial" sense.

If this was the sum total of things, what would be the point of creating a structure which has lasted billions of years for a sentient human being who could live for only a hundred years?

There would be no "temporal" sense.

If this was the sum total of things, what would be the point of creating a structure which is so complex, so exceptionally difficult to understand?

There would be no "cognitive" sense.

Man, blinded by his pride, might easily answer that all of this has no sense and above all there is no sense.

But this is really far too little.

The universe must not be seen in terms that are so banal and reductive.

The use of reason in the reaching of true knowledge.

We have already said that the optimal and almost exhaustive use of reason is to make us understand and adapt to the physical world in which we live.

But it is permissible to think reason could be something more than this.

A while ago I asked the Masters if reason, or more so, a rational approach, could be useful in the process of learning about true knowledge.

They told me our reason is particularly called upon when we find ourselves facing strange phenomena which are incomprehensible according to the mechanisms of the known physical world.

We think we already know everything, but at a certain point, unknown phenomena present themselves and, thanks to the spirit of investigation which they arouse, we make a small step forward in our knowledge which opens up a new world to us.

This is a constant mechanism in human history.

The unknown stimulates investigation which leads to new discovery and the experience of new knowledge. It is a simple evolutionary mechanism in the gradual awareness of creation.

Reason examines various possible theories to explain unknown phenomena.

Naturally the phenomena are strange for we human beings, but for those who have a wider view of things it does not appear to be a "phenomenal phenomenon" but can simply be read as a possible happening in a widened reality.

The presence of something strange pushes man on to make an effort to overcome his ignorance.

In other words, "unknown" phenomena are tools that have been deliberately introduced by Heaven to allow us to overcome our lack of understanding. Earth becomes a "stage" for these phenomena, as a base to act upon.

The incredible phenomena of the crop circles come to mind here.

The grain was used as a material base for writing a message[18]. There are also ancient stones on which indecipherable signs are written or which are shaped in incomprehensible ways.

The incomprehensible phenomena are signs which would like (I say "would like" because it is not taken for granted that they will achieve their aim and because firstly we have to understand them to receive their message) to transmit teachings which go beyond the physical dimensions and time of Earth. Principles which are valid independently from time or space.

These signs can suggest or help us use our instinct to understand ideas or limits or practical indications.

Their field of influence ranges over all knowledge.

The real sense of the presence of hidden things and of "phenomenal phenomena" is to help us overcome our ignorance and, by extension, they are tools made available to us in order to help us evolve.

We can identify a particularly advanced use of reason in a book by Daniel Chanan Matt, "*The essence of the Cabala*" [20].

---

18 In my second book I widely dealt with the argument about the crop circles. I explained their meaning as a message from "terrestrial-extras" who are trying to transmit knowledge to us which we obstinately refuse to understand. I have partially examined their way of coming about which moreover, is confirmed by a video that I was able to see after [11], and whose veracity was confirmed by expert specialists (e.g. by the criminologist and psychologist Dr Mauro La Porta, who I heard speaking at the IVth Congress of Divining and Radionics at Monteortone (PD) in November of 2008).

The book is a type of anthology of the writings of some of the great interpreters of the Jewish Cabala[19].

The Cabala or Qabbalàh or Cabbala is part of the esoteric tradition of Jewish mysticism especially the development of mystic thought in Europe starting from the 7th and 8th centuries A.D.

The Cabala[20] centres around the attempt to take a person back to the "cosmic awareness", or better, to a mystic union with God which humanity enjoyed before the fall into the awareness of good and evil[21].

Nothing could be more mystic and further from reason, I hear you say.

You would be wrong.

In fact the Cabala is a particular interpretation of the Jewish Bible or Tanakh and gained prominence with the publication of the book Zohar[22,23] (radiance).

Basically it says that the Torah, part of the Tanakh, is a codex which illuminates the mechanisms of Creation.

By being a codex and intelligible, it can largely be understood by reason.

In fact you need "great brain" with added memory and a lot of devotion to study in order to understand it.

The maximum expression of reason is required.

Reason helps[24] even at these high levels.

However, let us be frank, it is not something for everyone.

A fundamental part of the Cabala is synthesized in the "Tree of Life", a representation containing the "mechanisms" of creation and speaks about the origins of the physical universe as an emanation from the "Unimaginable".

---

19   In the appendix I have added some information on the Cabala to try to give a taste of its intrinsic wisdom.

20   In Hebrew, Qabbalàh (הלבק) is the act of receiving.

21   Do you remember Adam and Eve...?

22   The basis of the Zohar is due to a Spanish Jewish mystic, Moses De Leon, who wrote it through a form of channelling, as I am doing in the drafting of most of this book. My Masters told me that those of them who encouraged him were Masters of the highest level.

23   It was published around the 13th century A.D.

24   N.B. I say "help" because reason in itself is not sufficient.

The same Tree of Life also talks about the position of man in the universe.

Man is equipped with a mind through which he can exercise awareness[25]. The latter becomes the fruit of the physical world or better, the fruit of man's mind dropped into matter.

The Original Infinite Energy can experience and express itself in matter through a finite form.

After that the energy of Creation is condensed in matter, the Cabala argues that it has a rise along the path shown in the Tree of Life until it is united with its true and original nature again.

Much of what the Masters have told me can be found in these considerations from the Cabala.

As far as the discussion I am writing about is concerned, the role of the human mind and with it reason, stand out as an element of awareness.

The search for and the use of symbols.

In an attempt to identify a method of dealing with the symbols which bring true knowledge, I asked the Masters how I could carry out research which would allow me to understand them. They pointed out to me that in the passing of terrestrial epochs or in the development of "linear" time, much knowledge has been lost and only that written in books remains. In the distant past, there were men who were able to understand these messages from On High, transmitted by strange signs that certainly could not have been produced by man in the concept of human "possibility" of that time.

This understanding sprang from the interpretation of non-physical "trips" that these people made which allowed them to open the gates into man's lack of knowledge.

These beings were then capable of "memorizing" newly acquired

---

25 "The aim of a soul when it enters into a body is to show its strengths and actions in this world, to do so it needs an instrument. Descending into this world increases the flow of its strength to guide a human being through the world. Therefore it makes itself perfect above and below by reaching a superior state in which it can fully realize itself in every dimension. If it is not wholly fulfilled, be it above and below, it is not complete", Moses De Leon [7].

knowledge in material; in rocks, in sculpture and in architecture for example.

One of our possible methods of research could be to go back to these documents, this ancient memory of the interpretation of the phenomena. If we could recognize the message it would be easy to go back to the knowledge enclosed within and defeat current ignorance.

When I asked if I would be able to find the hidden truths in the books, I was told that some images and symbols contained in the books, if properly interpreted, could open the doors for me. At the same time They told me not to trust the interpretation of who had written the book.

I had to trust the "drawing" or the "image" not the written word. The graphic representation or the sculpture, drawing or symbol contains the correct message but the explanation given by man is generally mistaken.

When I asked if books such as those by Zecharia Sitchin [34] could contain knowledge which we are speaking about, They said only partly.

But, they made it clear that the Sumerian terracotta tablets with their cuneiform writings and drawings, referred to by Sitchin, were reliable points of research.

In fact, in my third book I had the good fortune to interpret one of these tablets, indeed a small terracotta prism which allowed me to obtain exciting results.

In the same discussion, I asked if the findings from Ancient Egypt could be a useful source of knowledge and they told me that many (but certainly not all) of the objects traced back to there could be useful in accomplishing the objective.

Of all of these objects, they told me to prioritise the "zodiac of Dendera", this was also analyzed in my third book, and in many ways came up with new results.

On other occasions They stressed that I had to have faith in the drawings and not give credit to the written explanations which currently interpret them.

Current wisdom should be revised and re-elaborated in the correct way discriminating between what is right and what is wrong.

Human knowledge is completely blind now and cannot distinguish between what is really significant and important and what is not.

They often asked me to stop believing in current thought which is mistaken and presumptuous at the same time and to "take wing" in both the literal and symbolic sense.

I have to, we have to look down from above and stop when and where our eyes are truly impressed.

When we look down from above, we are driven in the unique aim of incorporating things, which cannot be seen from close up, into a higher system of knowledge which is only achievable, and I repeat only, through agreement with those who live On High and those who live on Earth.

Men tend to neglect this higher knowledge, either because they do not see it directly or because they forget about it due to the immediacy of their everyday earthly activities.

I was absolutely banned from looking into the "underground tunnels" or, at a symbolic level, of studying knowledge that lacks illumination or does not come from them On High.

Those Up There really care about what is fundamental for the development of the Earth and the Universe, but man only manages to grasp this superficially, despite the best efforts of those on high.

Investigating further on my work methods, I was told that there is not only one method but several and not only one work but several.

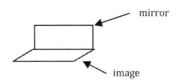

One of the first suggestions was to get hold of drawings and images and crop them at the point of interest and then look at them in the mirror.

Exactly as Leonardo had done, a character who is much appreciated On High.

He received information as it was actually sent from Up There and not as mirrored images on Earth.

Mirroring images allows us to straighten them and understand them correctly.

Another suggestion was:

"A step into the past and one into the future, but at the same time keep an eye on the radar. Betrayed by the present, knowledge and cosmic void escape us".

I understood that this meant that the "images" I had to find would come from the past (already existing structures, sculptures, objects and paintings etc) but also from the future, or at least from signs that speak of the future.

As far as this discussion is concerned, the latter clearly refers to the crop circles which must be correctly interpreted in order to identify what risks we are running.

Someone is trying to put us on our guard.

"Radar" means we must carefully consider types of karmic consequences (a type of mental "radar") regarding the planet Earth[26], as well as a series of magnetic[27] and gravitational[28] "manifestations" that will come about.

Man supposes that these last two are extraneous to the future and are seen as Earthly perturbations.

Man is so immersed in the present that he undergoes a sort of blackout in accessing the data that he needs most for his growth and survival. His behaviour makes it difficult for Those above to pass on knowledge and the

---

26 Even the Earth has its karma!

27 I sustain that the Masters allude to a gradual change in the intensity of the values of the Earth's magnetic field, something which could lead to an inversion of the magnetic poles. Clear reductions in magnetism have been detected instrumentally by specific monitoring which has been in place for some decades. According to Gregg Braden [6], the reduction in magnetism is linked to a slowing down of the rotational speed of the Earth, which has been measured experimentally. This is supported by measurement data which shows a variation of Earth's base resonance frequency (Shumann). This is a sort of electro-magnetic pulsation of the Earth which the human body is in harmony with, (this is artificially generated in astronauts, the consequences of its absence show a distortion in the body's natural biological rhythms).

28 The Masters pointed out that is about a forthcoming phase in the reduction of the intensity of the gravitational field.

"cosmic void" or the perception of the non-material parts of creation which he (man), sees simply as an "emptiness", a "nothingness".

The thought set of man is so resistant to understanding this, that Those above are obliged to send obvious signs to aid interpretation of the Earth's creation and the correct path to re-enter into its logic.

Man doubts and interprets this wrongly because he is so influenced by impure streams of consciousness.

They strongly advised me to take "Symbology"[29] on board as a research method.

The use of symbolic language is a considerable help which can do me no harm. There have been symbols since antiquity *"which do not obstruct those who wish to lift the veil of ignorance"*.

The Circle is the symbol which can help me most.

In the third book [4] I widely used and described it, identifying it as the most important of the 38 forming principles and catalysts of Creation, those which link Creation itself with the Creator.

The Circle is the possibility of connecting to and entering a relationship with Him.

Since we were not given the possibility of knowing the Creator, something which should be our maximum aspiration, our greatest possibility becomes one of being connected to him, and the Circle best represents this.

The sublime symbol.

The circle was the primordial shape which was followed in time by the "line" which "betrayed" the initial opening of knowledge and led us on a limited track.

The line is the symbol of man who is heavily limited at the moment of his "disconnection" from the Creator.

The meaning of this book is to teach us to go along an inverse path and to detach ourselves from the line to go back to the circle.

The understanding of the act of creation.

This is one of the main steps in the approach to true knowledge.

I have already suggested that it is not possible to know the Creator and consequently to know why the Creator decided to give life to Creation.

---

29   Look again at the meaning of "symbol" in note 2 of this text.

The aim remains unknown until at least we belong to Creation. But, at the time I was told that we human beings had to reach an understanding of the act of Creation. In fact I was told that this understanding constitutes <u>the fundamental knowledge</u> and the process of understanding is infinite.

Therefore, it is not a specific knowledge that can be acquired in a determined moment and end the discussion.

Rather, it is <u>the sense of the evolutionary path of human beings</u> and not only that.

We are here to gradually widen our knowledge of the act of Creation.

We are well aware that even Creation is not an instantaneous or momentary act which came about as one off occasion at the beginning of time, but is something continuous, a creative continuum which develops in the linear time which we find ourselves in.

These are really fundamental concepts and I fear that I am not capable of explaining their sense adequately with words.

Anyway, I will try my best.

An "effect of eternity" constantly inserts itself in our life, our physical life on Earth in linear time.

There is something beyond the time which we know, which continuously connects with our life. And it is this "effect" which generates a type of gradual and continual understanding of the act of creation.

This should not be confused with what is normally called "grace", or an illumination of the Catholic God *"who created everything in those famous seven days"*.

This statement from the Masters was communicated to me to let me understand that God as visualized by Catholics, and to Whom they attribute a fast and concentrated creative act, is in fact of man's creation and as such, is a God limited by man's scarce understanding.

We have to gradually reach an understanding of Something much bigger, a God that is much bigger than man's imagination.

We can only do this through the understanding of His act of Creation.

The path of creation lacks one fundamental fact: the understanding of the Divine Sign, which springs from God and began the Creation.

This sign becomes the creator of systems which are not only conceived or conceivable in the mind of man[30], but which are something much larger in which the *"energetic"* aspect plays a fundamental role.

A huge step towards the understanding of this divine sign was mentioned in my *third book* when I tried to interpret the deep meaning of the "zodiac of Dendera", a famous bas-relief on the ceiling of the central room of the East chapel of Osiris on the roof of the Temple of Hathor at Dendera in Egypt.

Fig 1: Photograph of the "zodiac" of the Temple of Hathor in Dendera.

One thing that clearly emerges is that the "zodiac" is not quite a zodiac, or even a more or less approximate representation of the astrological-

---

30   The systems conceivable by the human mind were defined at that time by the Masters as *"cerebral systems"*.

astronomical knowledge of the ancient Egyptians, it is much, much, much more.

It does not constitute a banal representation of human knowledge, but rather the representation of a message of knowledge from the edges of Creation, we might even dare to say from the Creator himself, through the connection that men[31] who lived thousands of years ago were able to make with him.

Calling it "zodiac" horribly diminishes its meaning, it was called this because it was not known what it was or maybe, no one dared to read its infinite depth which pervades it.

At that time I proposed to try to correct this serious mistake or to give it a new name, shared by the Masters, "THE GREAT MESSAGE OF DENDERA".

The bas-relief of Dendera was therefore a message that the Creator sent to the ancient Egyptians because they knew what creation was.

The "artistic" construction is admirable.

The central part describes the development of Creation, its history, seen through the knowledge and traditions of ancient Egypt.

Its "chaotic" portrayal intends to highlight its characteristic of apparent disconnection or of a relative or incomprehensible meaning of single events as seen through the eyes of those who live or recount them.

However, the ordered figures on the surround assure us that the apparent chaos of Creation is in reality straightforward and activated by clear and well-defined principles.

I called them the "*forming principles*" in my third book.

These figures, along with the Circle, which completes and unites them, descend from and are supported by the Creator, the Unknowable, unique depositary of the meaning of everything.

The admirable artwork is nothing compared to the general meaning of the message and the specific teachings it transmits. It teaches us that the ancient Egyptians knew the edges of Creation because they were in conscious connection with the Creator through the forming principle of the Circle and consequently they could know about the basis on which

---

31 The artist of the bas-relief summarized information from the numerous "enlightened men" of his epoch and preceding epochs.

Creation rested. In other words they were able to have a much wider vision of existence than the extremely partial and materially concentrated one that we have now.

The ancient Egyptians knew, for example, that terrestrials were not the only population of creation.

In the bas-relief of Dendera there is a clear reference to the population of Sirius in the first place and secondly to the people of two other constellations.

They also knew that their ancestors, and maybe not only ancestors, were beings from the stars or planets with Sirius at the top, so much so they considered their remote history to be the history of the people of Sirius.

Anyway, a great message which, in the part that interests us most i.e. the act of Creation, allows us to understand that the apparent chaotic development of universal life is contained in an order.

The ordered placing of thirty-seven figures on a circle portrays this.

The circle completes the discourse tied to the figures supported by it. It completes them in number and in the sense that, being distinct from them, in some way it portrays an element which is greater than them.

I was told that the figures represent a set of "shapes" similar to when you make a dessert and you put the almost liquid dough into a circular container and it comes out round and not square. The same thing is true for Creation.

It can only exist with those determined shapes and modalities.

Naturally, they are shapes that aren't only applied to the physical world but to all the components and dimensions of creation, in themselves they aren't "material shapes" but more like "energetic shapes" thus re-connecting us to what was said above regarding the fact that the divine sign is expressed in an "energetic" way.

Having said that, maybe a more correct word in the place of "shape" would be "matrix", or even better, "FORMING PRINCIPLES".

The bas-relief of Dendera shows us and describes the thirty-seven forming principles of Creation, connected to the Creator himself by the thirty-eighth principle, the circle, the forming principle which "connects Creation with the Creator."

This means that Creation can't be, have, contain or imagine anything which goes beyond these thirty-eight principles. Simply put, the existence of anything else in Creation isn't possible.

All of the possibilities of Creation are totally contained in the thirty-eight forming principles.

Knowing this means having the complete "manual" of Creation available, including its contents and its behavioural modalities.

I was also told that not only do the forming principles show us how creation came to be but that they also activate it!

It is a continuous activation not only done once and for all time.

Understanding the forming principles is the ultimate cognitive objective of every living being.

Their "experiential" understanding represents the evolutionary path of human beings, but not only human beings.

There is not one of the forming principles which regards knowing the Creator, nothing in Creation will ever be able to understand the Creator Himself no matter what religions and our mystic intuition or deepest esotericism tell us[32].

It cannot be done simply because the Creator has not inserted the possibility of doing so in our Creation.

However, the Creator has given us the possibility of being connected to Him, we can't know Him but through the CIRCLE we can have a relationship with Him[33].

The circle is the forming principle of this connection.

A duty of the few.

You will have understood by now, that reaching true knowledge is a gradual process, and in certain aspects, a process of breaking with current knowledge.

It is understandable then, that the "pathfinders" of this new knowledge can only be a few people who are capable of "overcoming" current thinking and not be conditioned by it. Opening the new way isn't for everyone.

---

32 Not even the highest spiritual entities of Creation can know the Creator.

33 I have been told that, in reality, we are always connected to the Creator, it's just that we don't know or are aware of it.

During the transfer of a beautiful message directly to a computer through A's fingers, the Masters said:

"There is always a nucleus of a few people, and certainly not the
mass, who carry forward this type of advanced knowledge. The
results, which are the fruit of an uncommon school of thought, were
brought into matter by special personalities such as the High Priests
of the Egyptians which they transferred into the pyramids.
They were capable of doing so because they were able to control their minds.
Therefore we will know, based on direct experience, that this advanced
knowledge will only help the best people to see beyond the limited
point of view of humans. Therefore the objective of identifying and
subsequently defeating ignorance is the duty of a few people".

I am honoured that the Masters have also chosen me as one of the few people to carry out this duty, which has fascinated me like nothing before in my life.

Italy is in the rearguard.

One day we were speaking about those few people who could be trusted with the duty of carrying forward the advanced knowledge, and we began to speak about Italy, which seemed to have a past of great contributions and innovations in knowledge.

Alas!

They answered ironically:

"Italy has this privilege. Italy has already done a lot in this sector, be it
respecting the opinion of the head of religious power or politically participating
in enterprises in space in which there is no real "in house" tradition."

Or, if we want to be serious, Italy has the "privilege" of having done too little by retreating too much in the face of false affirmations of knowledge.

And excessively respecting the opinion of religious power and at the same time participating in "scientific" enterprises in space, which among other things is not part of its tradition.

They also told me that Italy gives far too much importance to the material side of things.

Because of this, some terrestrial-extras[34], or better still, one of those characters, who resided in Italy[35], and who is trying to send us the messages of true knowledge which can help us, stated that maybe it is useless to give this country news which anyway, has already been transmitted elsewhere.

In Italy we find ourselves in a type of rearguard where the residue of the information that arrives lets us understand just how much we have lost of what was already known in countries such as Egypt.

It is not by chance, that in my third book I had to go "abroad" to investigate the ancient findings whose origins are very far from the Italian environment.

Outside help?

Without outside help it will be practically impossible for man to escape from the "impasse" which traps him.

As far as I'm concerned, the first help that the Masters are giving me is by consigning me the content of this book and those which have preceded it.

At the time, they told me:

> *"The rigidity of the human thought set will oblige Us to demonstrate the logic on which faith in the act of Creation of the planet Earth is based.*
> *And men, invested with less pure streams of knowledge, doubt, insert false contents, etc."*

Therefore, not only do the Masters help us, but They really feel obliged to do so.

They tell us that the men's minds are so reluctant to understand, that Those above are obliged to send us manifest signs to allow us to better understand the meaning of Earth's creation and the correct path that leads us back into its logic. That is why we humans, "infected" by streams of false

---

34 The Masters call those characters who live on Earth but are not "normal" human, terrestrial-extras.

35 It seems to me that the "brain drain" in Italy is not only limited to a strict scientific setting…

knowledge continue to doubt, err in our interpretations and make colossal misjudgements.

We aren't on the right road at all and we can't go on like this for much longer.

It is better that we begin to put our trust in someone external who is capable of giving us a hand.

The Masters identified extra-terrestrials from some distant corner of the skies as those who could help us.

There are some of them who really want to help us, however there are others who do not have the same benevolent approach towards humans.

In my "third book", I highlighted a significant example of these two differing behaviours.

I showed the positivity of those who helped the Tiahuanaco civilization[36] as opposed to the perverse strategy of those who "helped" the people of Nazca[37].

Obviously it is fundamental that we should be very careful who we put our faith in.

These extra-terrestrials have physically landed on Earth a few times, even although most of the encounters that they have had with terrestrials have been of a "mental" type in which the respective "material" parts are separated by a huge physical distance in the Universe.

There are many representatives of these people on Earth nowadays, physically present, some of them have peculiar physical characteristics while others are partially confused with human beings.

Their presence has been confirmed so often that to deny it is to close your eyes before the evidence.

But, the Masters told me that there are also others who can help us.

They defined them as terrestrial-extras.

In appearance they are like humans but they have something "angelic" about them which makes them "extra" compared to normal terrestrials. Their "wide vision" allows them to see "true knowledge" and their positive disposition towards humans means that they work for the well-being of man.

---

36 In the high plain of Bolivia, near Lake Titicaca.
37 In Peru.

Naturally, when the Masters told me about these human beings I thought it unlikely and my curiosity insisted on knowing more.

Who are they exactly?

Are they men or angels?

If they are men, what do they share with other common men?

How do they help other men?

There were many answers but an understanding of who they really are remained cloudy for certain aspects.

I'll try to shed some light on the subject.

They told me that there are two groups of "special" human beings on Earth. One group can be defined as "major" and the other "minor".

The human beings who want to help mankind belong to the major group and can be defined as "Earthly Angels". Their origins are completely human.

By saying "Earthly Angels", we want to underline

"The sound of the voice of those Angels",

which is light and true knowledge, is of Earthly origin.

The aspect relative to their Earthly origin is in complete contrast to the other terrestrial-extras "the minors" who would have us believe the idea of man "alone" with no connection to the rest of the Universe and with no help from a superior who knows who.

The latter is substantially the idea conveyed in the signs of Nazca[38] which doesn't want that a message of light and true knowledge could be of earthly provenance to be known.

A while ago the Masters had a long discussion with me on human beings and their souls.

---

38   In the third book I described how the signs of Nazca meant to convey the false idea of man "alone" in the Universe, with an aggressive feeling towards the outside, towards anything which is not human. Before, there had been "natural" contacts with these extra-terrestrials who were not considered hostile to man. Such a feeling was generated with the strategic end of the annihilation of man, indeed, to provoke his self-annihilation caused by the mistaken conception of his position and his aim in the world. Nazca represents the idea of *"Earth as a closed entity and with no possibility of connecting with the Spirit and a superior knowledge"*.

It came out that not all souls are equal.

It is as though there are different groups of souls, similar amongst themselves but different from other groups.

They made me an example of a chest of drawers, each drawer contains a certain type of clothing. One drawer has socks, another pants, another shirts, another hankies and so on.

The drawers put together contain the entire clothing of a person.

The analogy with the souls is easily explained: groups of similar souls exist and they have a pre-set objective and path in the setting of creation which is different from other groups.

But it is all the groups together which create the human species[39] and all of them are necessary for its evolution.

No human being is useless, but we can have different aims and in fact, can be very different.

So, the two groups of terrestrial-extras as defined above belong to two specific "drawers" of men's souls.

Both of them belong to more elevated drawers, to the category of "superior" men, however, they both have different aims and profoundly different behaviour towards other human beings.

As far as the "Earthly Angels" are concerned, they are by all accounts human beings, the most elevated of humans from an "energetic" point of view, they undergo few reincarnations but when they finish them, they become True Angels.

Their path is to "cure" the planet. It foresees that at a certain point, they leave matter (they leave Earth, or more so, they stop reincarnating) they abandon and free themselves from the mechanisms of Karma (also during the last reincarnations) and they are taken On High, but without negating the Earth and continuing to serve it by helping it through the use of its energy.

It is likely that the origin of their souls (their drawer) manages both their way of being human and also their contemporaneous path as angelic beings.

They are therefore a bridge between the physical world and the spiritual

---

39 In fact, this does not only refer to human beings but also to many other physical and non-physical "populations" of the Universe.

one … given that, although it is by no means certain, they are two distinct worlds.

These are the beings who send other humans the most autonomous messages, the truest that exist on the Earth and they are also the beings who are least likely to cede to the way of conceiving the Earth according to the "thinking of Nazca".

These are the human beings who we should listen to with a great deal of attention.

One of their ways of sending us messages is through the crop circles.

In my *second book*, I was interested in this phenomenon on more than a few times, for most people they are something absolutely incomprehensible and for others, the work of extra-terrestrials.

No!

The crop circles are messages which would be well worth decoding in a hurry.

They are caused by these "special" human beings who are endowed with a particular role and a particular connection with the spirit.

Therefore, we do not have to necessarily look for help from extra-terrestrials, even if an exchange with them will shortly become evident, there are men who can help other men!

These men are certainly a little special; think about it, they can transform themselves into angelic beings even during the incarnation.

It isn't that they abandon their physical body but they are capable of carrying out energetic "activity" from an angelic world.

For example, thanks to this connection with the spiritual plain, they are able to use their mind to literally organize plasmatic agglomerations which are visible at a physical level and to convey an idea and to mark it on a physical plain.

The crop circles are the physical results of these forms of "intelligent" plasma generated by the minds of these men.

The problem is that only one type of "plasma", that of the crop circles, is not enough to put man's ignorance in crisis.

Luckily enough, the terrestrial-extras are able to transform into various types of "plasma"[40] and to find better ways to reach man and force him to know[41].

Man's memory or what he had already discovered in the distant past does not help these terrestrial-extras to send their message as much as the "game" of coincidence does instead.

Though the action of the plasma can't be seen by man, it organizes happenings and tries to help people in a way that they must forcibly pass through new elements which for some, have no sense or never existed or are indecipherable[42].

"This help from the plasma becomes an extremely useful message for who receives it and provokes a huge mental opening for him. Why did I say that we need more than one type of plasma? We never before imagined that more than one kind existed and less so that they were present on Earth in the clothing of rescuers. But man needs them and therefore they come to Earth, but they do not give man anymore than he needs at that specific historical moment."

Now we know something more about who they are that can help us. Maybe it is opportune that we get to know them and understand their suggestions.

---

40 I fear that saying exactly what plasma is or what its various types are, sometimes so significantly different from that described by our scientists, would be an arduous task. I will leave this for more specialized moments. In the "second book" I add numerous details on this type of physical and non-physical phenomenon.

41 I think I am undergoing a notable "forcing" of this type at the moment, given all that they are making me write...

42 Do you remember the meaning of "strange and incomprehensible" phenomena described earlier?

Time and outside of time.

The concept of time merits discussion in the context of coming closer to true knowledge. Many illustrious men have grappled with this argument, quibbling philosophically, poetically or scientifically about it.

I want to add a different point of view, the way the Masters see it.

Everyone experiences the passage of time. It inexorably marches on, we are born, we grow up, we die without being able to stop it or turn it back.

The Masters call this "linear time" because it is like running along a line which is always there but only goes in one direction.

This kind of time makes us feel a little "limited", it's annoying not being able to turn back the clock, say thirty years, to when we were young, strong and beautiful.

It's also a nuisance that we can't go forward in time to see our future twenty years from now and then come back to the present to modify our behaviour so that "little problems" now don't become "disasters" twenty years later.

Time forces us to live in the present.

This doesn't go down well with many people.

Their mind continually harks after the past with all its relative beauty and even "heaviness", or to project themselves to a hypothetical future, potentially beautiful, but completely imaginary and with no guarantee of becoming real.

In other words, in this kind of time, the past is no more and the future has still to arrive.

Our perception of time and its use is made up of many moments of the "present".

Is it limiting or our good luck that it is so?

I don't know, but if the Creator made it like this, there must be a reason behind it.

Can we know more?

Let's try and find out.

In my *second book* the phrase which I used at the beginning to sum up its content or maybe as a good luck omen, was:

"*God gave us time so we could understand Him,*
and love so we could return to Him".

That sentence, which came from some thoughts sent by the Masters, not only had meaning for that book, but has a meaning that speaks volumes: it contains the path of Creation. In other words, "time" and "love" are the main instruments of Creation.

Firstly, time, means that the Creator, who is "outside of time", decided to begin Creation and with it, time[43].

Be aware that "outside of time" where the Creator is, is not eternity, which is already another form of time, it is a place where time doesn't exist at all.

By saying that "*God gave us time so we could understand Him*" means that the Creator activated the Creation with the instrument of time.

Creation is the setting where the process of understanding the Creator has to be developed.

Creation can be seen as a "laboratory" of experiences which are developed in time and which gradually lead us to an understanding of Creation itself and through that, an understanding of the Creator.

I know that I'm risking going over your heads … please show some understanding, trying to arrive at true knowledge requires a real effort sometimes.

Once Creation has been understood, the next step is to return to the Creator through love, the other great instrument of Creation.

What exactly is love? … we shall see further on.

---

43   The title of a book by Cioran "The fall into time" [9] comes to mind here. Is Creation a temporary "fall into time" from which we arise and return to the Creator? Is it that Cioran himself imagined this return as a second fall. The "fall from time" or otherwise the end of History?

For the moment let's limit ourselves to time.

As I have already mentioned, time isn't only the linear time that we're used to. Linear time as we know it, is a very limited concept, much the same as our limited concept of matter.

Just as a type of continuity and gradualness exists in matter, from the ethereal of the most elevated spiritual beings to the most solid of the physical plain, time works using the same analogy.

We can therefore say that there is a sort of continuity and gradualness between the maximum expression of time which we can identify as an "eternity which is globally and contemporaneously present"[44], and the minimum expression of time that is our linear time.

The fact that linear time isn't always understood as an objective passing of minutes and seconds, began to be highlighted by the "squarest" of scientists.

When that "tear-away" Einstein[45] got it into his head that time passes differently if we are calmly seated on our couch than when we are travelling at the speed of light, then obviously we aren't sure anymore that there is only one type of time.

But rather than discomfort scientists, let the person who has never perceived the existence of "different time" cast the first stone.

Do you perceive time in the same way when you are bored, or making love with your partner, or when you are dreaming?

This is only an act of perception you may say, time is marked by the clock.

But don't be so sure about that I say, and not only me ... but also the Masters.

I fear that I may begin to create some confusion for you.

But, once again, I ask you to be patient.

True knowledge requests a revision of the restricted concepts that our lives in the physical world have got us used to taking for granted.

---

44 My mind cannot go beyond this expression...

45 Before Einstein and his theory of relativity, it was always tacitly admitted that the attributions of time in an event would have an absolute value. Relativity forced the matching of these attributions to the state of movement of the reference body, meaning that a stationary person "sees" the passage of time differently from a person in movement. It only becomes evident by the difference of speed from the order of size of the light and therefore it passes unseen in our normal life [13].

Some time ago the Masters told me:

"Your era has thousands of years.
Ours is eternity.
Outside of time".

They wanted to highlight that man conceives time in a certain way, in terms of millennia and in fact, the human condition is normally thought about in these terms.

A temporal crumb compared to universal time or classical "geological time".

They mean that Their "time", other than not being momentary or brief, is something more compared to the linear time used on Earth.

It is a temporal "superset", it is bigger and more extensive than our own concept of eternity, which for us is nothing more than an infinitely long time.

Their "time" is a time which is confused with Creation itself, at that level it is no longer possible to separate the concept of time from, for example, matter or energy, it is whole, complete, it is The Time, it is The Creation, it is a phenomenal phenomena that the Creator wanted to be recognized.

All of the above is needed to relativize how much we currently think and to make it clear that our concept of time, like many of our other ways of seeing and conceiving existence, is only a fragment of something much, much wider.

It is a reassertion, starting from time, of our limited vision and of the necessity to expand it to gradually reach true knowledge. If we remain in our limited and often mistaken vision, we close ourselves off from the possibility of advancing along the path we have been asked to take.

The Time we are talking about is close to the concept of a contemporaneous presence of all times and as a consequence of all places, situations and people, it is a type of omnipresence, both temporal and spatial, it is one of the qualities we normally attribute to God.

It's difficult for us as human beings to imagine such a situation even although we experience it in one way or another.

The main obstacle in understanding the above is our persistence in seeing the mind as the only possible "device" of knowledge.

As it is, the mind can only analyze one thought at a time, when it tries to consider more, it creates confusion and drives us crazy, in fact people who try to mix different thoughts relative to different situations at the same time are usually considered to be mentally ill.

The mind can only correctly analyze multiple thoughts if they are treated in sequence one after the other, or at best putting together a series of fragments of thoughts, alternating one piece of thought with another and then going back to the first.

But generally, this is rather stressful.

Therefore, our mind has a sequential way of working in perfect line with the concept of linear time that we are so used to[46]. When someone departs from this way of thinking, they are inevitably considered mad or mentally disturbed, because in general, if we only use our mind, we cannot conceive that there could be something that functions differently from it.

Our mind is perfectly aligned to our being in the physical world and our linear time.

But, here we are trying to understand that it could be much more in every sense: in the cognitive tools, going beyond the mind, in material-energetic dimensions, going beyond the physical world, in temporal dimensions, going beyond linear time.

The sentence quoted above says much more.

By saying *"Ours is eternity. Outside of time"* the Masters mean that their temporal environment is eternity and they are contemporaneously inside time and also "outside of time".

This means that they are contemporaneously inside Time or the Creation and also outside Time or in that Something which is outside Creation: The Creator.

And the real surprise is that we are contemporaneously in Creation and in the Creator!

I doubt if what I am saying is understandable to our mind.

I am not only saying that we belong to all of Creation, which is already something that goes far beyond our physical dimension and is only partially understandable to us, but I am also saying that contemporaneously we belong to or are in the Creator.

Our rational mind cannot understand this because it is not predisposed

---

46 I want to make it clear that by "mind" I mean a synonym of "rational knowledge". My meaning is strongly reductive of what the mind is or can be in reality, but I am referring to what we normally think it is.

to do so, indeed, to do its work well, which is to favour our physical life, it does everything it can to impede access to the "superior" dimensions. If we want to get closer to the "true knowledge", which belongs to these "superior dimensions", we have to try to escape from this closed environment, from the prison that our mind is.

As Huxley said we have to go through the "doors of perception" that our mind keeps us closed behind.

The door of the perception of time is also between these doors.

The transmission of information in linear time and "widened" time.

We have already seen what linear time means, or more over, the time we are used to perceiving as humans.

Man has adopted different strategies to pass on information through the generations.

The first strategy was to hand down knowledge from father to son.

When man started to use language this became known as "oral transmission". This method was useful but it had one huge defect, if the repository of knowledge died before passing it on, it became lost.

When man became aware of this risk he made an effort to find new criteria and it is more than likely that writing was born as a result of this problem.

In my third book I talk about how the Sumerian cuneiform language, the most ancient known to us[47], was developed immediately after the universal deluge when the survivors noted that they had lost so much information that had previously been passed down orally and had disappeared with the death of the repositories.

Writing and the word, both "created" by our mind[48] on the basis of the same way of functioning, also have the same limits as the mind, they are forced to "brutally" synthesize, thus losing a myriad of information about the phenomena they wish to talk about.

---

47 According to scholars, its origins came about at least 5,000 years ago, in "my" opinion its origins came about shortly after the deluge around 7,300 years ago.

48 N.B. Word meant as a linguistic codex and writing are creations of our mind, while language or the possibility of communicating, comes from Someone from a higher level compared to human beings.

Furthermore, there is also the risk of misinterpretation when the meaning attributed to a word is different between writer and reader.

I recently read a book titled "The Black Swan" [35] which talks about how improbable it is to govern our life.

It talks about the *"Black Swan"* as *"an isolated, unforeseeable event of huge impact that our mind tends to justify afterwards".*

The writer, Taleb maintains that a *"small amount of black swans are behind every upheaval in history and are able to explain almost all of our world".*

"But we only notice this phenomena after it has already happened".

"And that is why our nature (read mind) *tends to learn from experience and repetition.*

We are hypnotized by the particular and lose vision of the universal.

We systematically neglect the things we don't know, we bow to the impulse to simplify, tell, categorize and go along already well trodden paths, rendering ourselves incapable of thinking the "impossible" which, in fact, governs our existence".

The book makes the idea clear that our mind is a reductive instrument and substantially supported on things we already know.

It is an instrument which is based on past happenings in the linear time of the human mind.

It is a really useful and indispensible instrument for life on Earth, but, all things considered, it is very limited.

Therefore a limited mind produced a limited word and writing, we find ourselves dealing with instruments of the same level.

The communicative strength of the symbol is very different.

As I have already said before, the symbol is a conduit which links us to what it represents, a certain "truth" or a "phenomenon" in its togetherness.

The symbol, unlike the word, globally communicates what it represents and is not forced to synthesize its meaning.

Of course the symbol no longer works only at the level of the mind, but goes on to a much wider dimension.

It is thanks to this "widening of the communicative spectrum" that what is transmitted is much richer and deeper than the word.

We are aware however, that some words or characters are symbols in themselves and therefore are great communicative vehicles.

As far as I know, one of the languages with an important symbolical content is Hebrew.

In its origins, every single character was a symbol completely capable of conveying a single event.

And when a word is composed of more characters, it not only contained the meaning of the word as happens in our modern languages but a type of sum of the symbolic meaning of all the characters, the single word, in itself, became a "bigger" symbol.

At this point let me insert a piece of "news" that really excited me the first time I read it.

There is a book by Sibaldi [33] which speaks about ancient Jewish angelology as it is passed down to us through the Qabbalah, and which in turn goes back to the book of Exodus and the ancient Egyptians. Three well-known verses from Exodus XIV relative to the parting of the sea that allowed the Israelites escape from the Egyptians, are here quoted.

XIX - "The Angel of God, who preceded the caravan of the Israelites, changed places and from the front passed to the rear. The column of clouds also passed from the front to the rear."

XX - "So it came to find itself between the file of the Egyptians and the caravan of the Israelites. The clouds darkened the way for the former, while, for the latter, the night was illuminated. Therefore the Egyptians could not get close to the Israelites all night."

XXI - "Moses stretched out his hands on the water. And during the night, the Lord drove back the sea with a strong Eastern wind, making it dry. The waters separated."

Well then!

In the Hebrew version, each of the three verses has exactly seventy-two letters and in Jewish angelology there are exactly seventy-two Angelic Powers[49] which, from now on, we shall call Angels.

All of the names of these seventy-two Angels are written with five

---

49 Here it would be opportune to study what an Angel is and what an Angel Power is according to Jewish angelology, because I am sure it is not exactly what you think it is. But for now I'll refer you to the illuminating book of Sibaldi [33].

letters, the first three represent the name of the Angel, while the last two represent one or the other of God's two main names.

Some names end in ה י (-yah), comes from Yahweh and others with ל א (-'el), comes from 'Elohyim.

So, remembering that Hebrew is written from right to left, if we take the first letter from verse XIX, the last letter of verse XX, and the first of verse XXI we have the name of the first Angel Wehewuyah.

Then, if we take the second letter of verse XIX, the second last of verse XX and the second of verse XXI, we have the name of the second Angel, Yeliy'el.

If we take the third letter of verse XIX, the third last of verse XX and the third of verse XXI we have the name of the third Angel, Seyita'el.

And so on, until we have the names of all seventy-two Angels.

Interesting, isn't it?

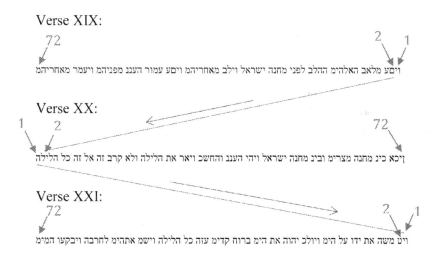

Verse XIX:

Verse XX:

Verse XXI:

Figure 2: the three verses of Exodus XIV which exactly represent the names of the seventy-two Angelic Powers of Jewish angelology.

But it doesn't end there.

Going back to the discussion that every single Hebrew letter is a symbol and therefore represents something well defined, the set of the three letters that compose the name also represent something well defined, reconstructed to start from the meaning of the single letter and from the way they are put together.

The path of the individual Angel is represented in his Name[50], the particular energy that he is able to pass on and the specific action he influences on the people who are associated with him or who turn to him.

Therefore, knowing the meaning of our Angel's name could "rationally"[51] illuminate our path, but the fact of being connected with the symbol behind the name allows us to "intuitively" understand His "energy" and the "angelic path" which he represents.

And it is the latter that is a "complete" connection, not "synthesized", as our reductive mind would allow us.

It is information that is gathered from outside linear time.

The symbol is a way of communication that works in a "widened" time.

Time and timing.

Some months ago, the Masters passed this message on to me.

It is something that I have already partially told you:

> "Let's take each other by the hand and go down
> together through the archway of time.
> The question of a certain type of Time becomes "timing" and
> NOW is the moment in which we have to highlight the way and
> arguments which must not be confused with the grace of that Catholic
> God who created everything in those famous seven days".

By this, I understood that the Masters intended and still intend to give me a hand and to go with me on my journey.

We will go down to the domain of Time together, or better, a "widened" temporal domain, well beyond time of men on Earth, the linear time that we know.

A special aspect tied to this Time becomes "timing" or, in other words, the right moment (hour and date) to fulfil something on Earth.

---

50 Hebrew tradition insists on capital letters.

51 It is information in linear time.

That "becomes" refers to something that happens in "widened" time, an act of the past, the present and the future.

Timing substantially becomes a link between this Time and a specific event in linear time: to give an idea, it is as if an "eternity effect" is inserted into our life.

In this precise moment of our time, what I am doing together with the Masters is dealing with themes on how things should be done according to a specific request from Time.

This "connection" is indeed something strange and special compared to what normally happens to men, it must not be confused with what is usually called "grace" or a gift, an illumination from the Catholic God "who created everything in those famous seven days".

This underlines that the Catholic God is not the Real Creator, but a God created by man. With our humanly pride we managed to create a God whose image is what we think God should be, an image which does not coincide with what God really is.

The true image of God must come down from Him and not from the human mind, which in its limitations, cannot presume to know Something, which in Itself is infinitely superior.

Time which becomes timing tells us that now is the right moment to gain access to a more correct vision of God and Creation, the right moment to enter into true knowledge.

Our current path in understanding consists of facing specific themes and trying to evolve their comprehension and finally to condense, understand and summarize their deepest meaning.

This is what I am trying to do thanks to the collaboration of the Masters and the books They advise me to read.

This is the action required of me by Time which becomes timing.

The work of the Masters.

The Masters are spiritual beings with a vision that is enormously wider than ours.

This work would not be possible without their help.

Their presence and the help they give us is perfectly placed in the general process of the evolution of Creation. We must experiment with matter, in the spirit They give us advice, guidance and protect our deeds.

It is teamwork, They need us and we are lost without Them.

The necessity of new knowledge.

A while ago the Master told me:

> "… my health, in terms of health on a superior level, requires me, us to insert a certain amount of information into man's understanding".

It is obvious that there is a clear necessity for Him to introduce human understanding to "correct information" because Heaven is "suffering" from something that is not going well on Earth.

We are not talking about collaboration between Heaven and Earth, but rather, a union whose aim is to improve the "state of health" which has been lacking.

The main problem is that man cannot feel good if he goes on maintaining that he cannot control or guide things that happen. The first step to resolve this problem is the introduction of new knowledge to man.

Opinion is divided in Heaven.

The Master's willingness and availability to help man is something that is not generally well thought of in Heaven.

He told me:

"I decided to "blame" the decisions of over saturation and primness made by others, while the Earth or the planet Earth no longer has confidence only in itself either for its own survival or due to the margins of error already committed in the past by men whose brains are more obtuse than ever".

By this He means to say that He is convinced that He has to highlight the mistaken decisions of other Heavenly Beings who retained that They have to exploit to the maximum the fact of making man believe that he could only trust himself regarding the survival of Earth and by breeding behaviour that is only positive in appearance.

Earth and men on Earth can no longer have confidence in themselves neither for the survival of the planet nor for the by now limited residual margins that have been caused by past mistakes by men who lacked a broad vision.

I conclude from this that there are contrasting opinions between Heavenly Beings as to how the human race should evolve on Earth.

The prevalent opinion up till now has been to leave man to what he best believes in.

But maybe by leaving him the possibility of self management in his supposed uniqueness and isolation from the rest of Creation has not produced the results desired in Heaven.

Man, left to his own devices, has lost his objectives and is losing the bets against himself.

It is at this point, with things going badly, that someone in High, like our Master, decided to change direction and give a hand in readdressing a situation which has been rather compromised.

In my book [4] I spoke about another people from the universe, the Poulrag.

In their journey through life they trusted their own ideas of life and the universe.

Things went rather bad for them however.

First, they destroyed the planet where they lived, due to causes which we would say were "natural". Then they were almost completely wiped out by a deluge while they were refugees on Earth near the area of Mesopotamia.

The Masters told me that the Bible was right in a certain sense when it described the destructive deluge as "divine decree" to wipe out the "corrupt and violent".

The destruction, indeed the repeated destruction of that people was caused by the fact that they did not know how to ally themselves to the sense, aim and meaning of Creation.

They were cut off from a connection with the Creator and they were following a road that was shown by their mind but not the one requested by Who had created them.

Whoever is not in line with Creation is no longer needed by It to achieve Its objectives and is destined to disappear.

The Masters want to tell us:

"Man, be careful!
Did you see what happened to the Poulrag!?
You are running the same risk."

We too, no longer being connected to the Creator, have distanced ourselves from the sense of Creation and if we go on like this we will not be part of the "Great Aim" and we will be eliminated.

Take care not to read this as an alarmist message sent by a bellicose and vindictive God, it is the absolute opposite, it is simply a message of good sense.

Those who are outside the aim of Creation have no reason to exist and shall be removed.

This is a general law of Creation and it is applied in all fields: those who are not part of a determined aim, regress or disappear sooner or later.

Darwin, in his theory of the evolution of the species thought the same way.

The mechanisms of modern economics cannot escape from it and human psychology is likewise subject to it.

I am writing this today because the Masters are trying to avoid the disappearance of the human race and the Earth in general. We absolutely have to reconnect to the Creator and rediscover and realign ourselves to the Sense and someone can help us.

The Masters are helping us, we only have to listen to them for our part.

The passing on of information.

The great "hand" that the Masters are giving man is through the passing on of information which, by its nature, cannot be gathered and accepted by just anyone.

They told me:

> "The first act of my intervention will be to pass on information
> and superior knowledge to some high level men.
> Then I will make the Spirit intervene in their destinies to
> safeguard their life, and thus safeguarding the fundamental
> Knowledge that I inserted in them first."

Therefore, not only information, but also a sort of "protection" from the Spirit to guarantee that the repositories of this new knowledge have the possibility, through a sufficient physical existence, to "exploit" the acquired information.

They also said:

> "There is always a nucleus of few people, and certainly not the great
> mass of men, who carry this type of advanced knowledge forward.
> And the results [...] are made into matter by special people
> [...] capable of controlling their thought set."

Only a few special people are "predisposed" to get this uncommon information.

One of the fundamental characteristics of these people is their ability to control their own thought set.

Do we have any idea what it means to control your own thought set?

I don't think it's even clear what thought set is ...

Thought set and thought.

Maybe it is time we dedicated some words to this fundamental aspect of the affair.

Exactly defining what "thought set" is, is not easy. We could simply say it is a "set of someone's thoughts", it could be a man or another being endowed with the ability to think.

But that is not enough, if it were only thoughts or ideas, some more, some less imaginative, everything would end there, leaving us little to talk about.

The big "thing" behind this is the fact that (and it is not normally clear to us) this thought set is endowed with an energetic capacity capable of provoking or impeding change.

We should get into the idea that a "thought provokes an action".

This is fairly obvious from a certain point of view, and many philosophers have seen thought as the basis of action, without arriving at the excesses of someone who saw thought as existence itself[52].

It is clear to all of us that to do something, we first have to think about it.

As a planning engineer, I know fine well that before I can realize any structure I have to plan it, or more so think about it.

In this sense it is obvious that thought is at the base of the realization of things in the material world.

But when I say that "thought provokes action" I mean something more.

---

52 Remember the famous "I think, therefore I am ..."

Above all it means that there is an energetic content. More than anything, thought is *"an energy in movement"*.

If you tell me I am right it is because you are well aware that when you think you get tired, and therefore you have consumed energy[53]... we still haven't got to the point of what I want to tell you.

Here I really mean to tell you that thought itself is an effective energy which is moving, and whether we want it to or not, will do something, a certain work, it will provoke movement or change.

Thought energy is really similar to muscular energy which allows us to hammer our finger (and do ourselves harm) or sexual energy which allows us to make love with our partner (and at times do ourselves a power of good!).

Einstein convinced us, with some difficulty given that we are not always sure, that matter is energy and vice versa.

I would like to convince you that thought is energy ... even although I fear it will be a much harder task than that done by the good Albert.

Believe me, in fact believe what the Masters tell me: thought is an energy, and also rather powerful.

If we can manage to see thought as an energy or as something which can produce a certain type of work, we can immediately draw on a whole set of considerations.

The disciplines which normally study energy and work are in the field of engineering.

The first "silly" consideration that we can make is that we can immediately include psychology and sociology in the engineering disciplines.

Does that seem strange?

If thought is energy and energy is the attitude to carry out a job, then there is not an engineering science that is more important than psychology, which studies the thoughts of the individual and their effect/work, or sociology which studies the thoughts of human groups and their effect/ work!

---

53 By the way, are we sure that we are clear what we mean by "energy"? As a good engineer I'll tell you what I learned at university, even if it is in a precise technical context, but I think the idea comes across well also in a general sense: " *energy is the attitude to carry out a job* ". Many types of energy can exist ... but that is another discussion.

Joking apart, the implications that thought is a powerful energy are immense.

I think the massive destructive power that thought can have is clear to everyone.

Think about how an individual can be destroyed by a nervous breakdown[54] generated by a single recurring thought or how a people can be destroyed by the delusions of grandeur (this is also a thought) of a leader.

Or vice versa.

What disturbing force was introduced into history by the thought of that great Spiritual Being known as Jesus?

Thoughts capable of conditioning human behaviour for millennia.

One could guess that different types of thought exist by looking at the few examples above.

Some of these thoughts are internal to people but essentially condition their life.

Even if these thoughts have little energy at the start, their continual repetition gradually gathers more strength through time. The sum total of many small energies creates something much bigger.

Another important aspect now comes into play, if thought is energy, the latter must come from somewhere.

The effect can be disastrous if a pounding thought continuously sucks energy from a person by its constant repetition.

Leaving aside nervous breakdowns[55] caused by banal self-destroying thoughts, people have also had breakdowns trying to determinedly carry out important projects.

The energetic mechanism of the thought is what I really want to highlight.

If it is energy, then it must come from somewhere!

Nothing creates nothing, or so I have been told.

---

54 Is this not the result of a gradual energetic subtraction operated by the thought's need for energy so that it can continue to repeat itself?

55 I retain that it is not currently known exactly what it is. This is a generic term to indicate that one no longer has the mental residue to continue living normally, but how a person arrives at this state of breakdown is generally known only through a description of the superficial mechanisms.

It doesn't take much to imagine that this energy could come from food or sleep.

But not only this, in fact there is a lot to be said about sleep.

It is normally thought that sleeping or resting recharges our batteries, if only by dint of the fact that at rest we are motionless.

But that does not make much sense.

It is like saying that by leaving our car in the garage, the petrol will increase in the tank. It is something I have hoped for many times but I'm still waiting for it to happen!

Nonetheless we are sure that our energy has increased after a good sleep.

Therefore, there has to be a top up of energy during our sleep, petrol is put in our tank.

Indeed, during sleep we go into a "modified state of consciousness", in which, apart from entering into the "well known" world of dreams, of which there is much to be said, but maybe later, we are much more predisposed to absorbing the energy we need to live and live well, than when we are awake.

What energy are we talking about?

It is an energy that is not known to modern science.

In fact, instead of talking about energy in the singular, we should talk about energies.

We can also add the adjective "subtle" to these energies so as to distinguish them from the "heavy" energies i.e. those which are normally measurable in the physical world.

The heavy/subtle distinction has a very precise meaning in identifying the concept of gradual change in the state of "density" of matter/energy.

In this sense we can say that matter is very "densified" and it is easy to understand the concept of gradual change if we think, for example, of the variants between the density of a rock and air.

Energies follow similar criteria.

We can identify a heavier energy and go all the way through to a lighter or less dense one.

We can classify the measurable energies of our physical world from the heaviest to the lightest[56].

---

56   I am aware that a modern physicist would turn his nose up at this statement …

The following list shows a similar classification of known energies.

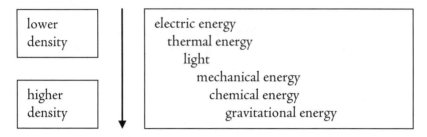

| lower density | electric energy
thermal energy
light
mechanical energy
chemical energy
gravitational energy |

higher density

Up to this point it is clear.

Now we penetrate something which is similar to the concept of a gradual reduction of density, but from which we cannot have answers on how to measure it, at least not direct answers.

We are in the field of subtle energy.

Due to the fact that we cannot measure subtle energy with "physical" instruments, we find it hard to admit their existence and we have constructed heaps of scientific theories which negate it[57],[58] or which do not take it into consideration.

But they exist, and how!

Many ancient traditions have identified some of them and they have also learned to frame some of their action mechanisms and use them.

This would be an interesting discussion to take up, but for the moment let's limit ourselves to saying that these "subtle" energies exist and that they have a sort of continuity in the variations of their density, reaching such levels of "rarefaction" as to seem empty (and that is if we limit ourselves to looking at them only from a point of view of the physical world in which we think to find ourselves).

---

but we are trying to find a new knowledge!

57 I don't remember where I read, *"even though the dialectic is allowed to subvert the truth, it nonetheless still remains in reality"*.

58 In the "Black Swan" [35] I read with great pleasure the considerations on our great ability to *"err with infinite precision"* (…almost a definition of our scientific culture) and on the great ability of human beings to demonstrate their vision of the world by looking for and identifying in the physical world, only those exact proofs which confirm that vision. It is a mental mechanism that is defined in the book as *"naive empiricism"*.

The discussion is not limited on the variations of density (a concept correctly applied especially to the world of matter), but also partially takes place in the field of variations of frequency, as well as dimensional transfers[59], which are also characterized by a smooth continuum.

For the moment let's be happy in the knowledge that there are many levels and great quantities of these subtle energies around us and that we need them to live: our body exchanges them with the outside.

There is a continuous exchange between our body and these energies, it is just that our normal wakened condition puts us in a state in which the balance between what we acquire and what we consume favours the latter[60], with the result of an increase in tiredness and the subsequent need to sleep or rest.

A simple rest already improves the acquisition/consumption relationship in favour of the former, but it is really during sleep that it is maximized, and the type and quality of energy acquired is widened.

In terms that are a little more difficult, but I think comprehensible, we can say that the "modified" condition that we find ourselves in during sleep allows a greater dimensional penetration or that we can avail ourselves of energy tanks that are present in dimensions that are not accessible in our wakened condition.

Meditation is another powerful tool that helps us to access these levels, despite being partially awake, it can contemporaneously open doors that are otherwise closed.

Crossing these thresholds allows us to enter places (that are part of our deepest selves as well as "reserve-tanks" that are available to everyone and everything) in which the acquisition of energy and more becomes possible.

---

59 It has always appeared logical to me to consider the "non-locality" phenomena found in the studies of quantum physics as journeys through different dimensional levels. In the classic study of the electron that suddenly passes from one energy level to another (around the nucleus of the atom), it has not yet been understood what it does during the transfer. In my opinion it seems plausible to admit that the electron gradually passes into another dimension invisible to us before returning to a dimension that is instrumentally measurable.

60 Our body can either consume or deteriorate some kinds of energy, or modify their quality in the sense of a worst possibility of use.

This is where the great relaxing and regenerating effect of meditation comes from[61], in a certain way it is very similar to sleep.

Let's go back to thought set.

I have strayed off line a little in the last few pages, in the sense that, talking about what the thought set is, I deviated and started talking about thought and its connection to energy, then going on to explain what this energy is and how it can be acquired, especially when we sleep.

Trying to take up the thread of the argument let me repeat that thought is energy and as such is capable of generating a certain type of work.

Our thought set is the environment where these thoughts generate, where they demand energy to develop and from where they start an action, or better, their energy begins to work.

But there is much more.

Our thought set, and that of others, is capable of connecting with the thought sets of other beings thus giving place to stronger and more active thoughts/energies.

Thought shapes, agents of illness.

I remember an interesting book by Anne Givaudan called "Thought shapes" [14].

Thought shapes are a particular effect of thought.

This is clearly highlighted as our thought set gives way to a particular "energetic manifestation" precisely defined as "thought shape".

These are not simple thoughts, they only show themselves in people endowed with the ability to reason, we can define them as "energetic globules" that move around us and are made up of and nurtured by certain recurring thoughts of ours.

---

61 Meditation can mean many things and there are many different techniques, they are not all equal and not all of them have the same effect. There are different levels of profundity, that are reachable through training and that allow a gradual increase in the state of dimensional penetration. The subject of meditation is very wide and would merit discussion on its own.

The more we "think" about them, the more we nurture them energetically and the longer they live.

For example, an obsessive thought is a typical thought shape that is rather strong and is recognized as a cause of alteration in our psychological well-being.

However, it is also right to say that not all thoughts generate thought shapes: "*for this to happen there has to be something major in our life which is expressed in strong emotions. And this shape lingers and amplifies itself if there is a repetition or, faced with similar events, the subject continues to react or think in the same way*".

There are many thought shapes, some stronger than others, but they all share a fixed trait: they are based on our more or less deformed and personalized way of seeing reality.

In short, they are distortions of our vision and way of facing life in general, and consequentially generate energetic agglomerates which are not "clean" and are harmful to our wellbeing.

As well as producing an alteration in our psychic well-being, they can also modify and disturb our energetic bodies and end up provoking physical illness.

Nowadays, it is quite taken for granted by doctors in the field of psycho-analysis to attribute the responsibility for many illnesses defined as "psychosomatic" to certain recurring thoughts, but the mechanism that generates these is still unknown and above all, they deny the fundamental energetic effect of thought that I have been trying to explain.

The Masters tell me to specify that it is not only psychosomatic illnesses that are generated by thought, but all illnesses, and I mean all illnesses, are generated by thought shapes and, strange as it may seem, so are all accidents.

What has been said can help understand the enormous influence that thoughts generated by the thought set can have on a person.

These thought shapes, this mass of mostly "dirty" energy has the possibility of "travelling" in space and connecting with similar shapes from others to constitute "maxi" thought shapes that are defined in technical terms as "egregore".

In [24] the egregore are described as *"firstly a motor, a mass of energy nurtured by all thoughts of a similar kind which circulate on the Earth's surface"*.

An egregora is a thing that does not have a life of its own[62] but is fed by the thought shapes of many; therefore as long as it is thought about, it lives.

The problem is that if many people generate the same thought shapes that then form an egregora, the latter will have the energy of many and could become a very powerful "thing", capable of influencing people who, at the beginning, have nothing to do with it.

The strange thing is that it is energetically nurtured even by those who resist it.

Let me show you a simple example.

You know that the question of abortion is divided into two warring camps; pro-abortion and anti-abortion.

In the United States these positions are fiercely fought and in recent years, almost all of the doctors who practice abortion (almost always on medical grounds, even if illegally) after the eighth week of pregnancy, have been murdered.

This news particularly shocked me.

How can a person, who has the absolute conviction to defend life, even in its non-mature and initial stage, come to kill an adult human?

An absurd blind fanaticism, you may say.

And I could say you are right, but that explanation isn't sufficient.

I maintain that basically there is an energetic mechanism explainable with thought shapes and egregore.

The abortion problem, by its strongly emotive nature, has certainly generated many thought shapes and "distorted" thoughts for example, in the women who have accepted undergoing a termination of their pregnancy.

It is a type of problem that closely interests almost all human beings.

---

62   If I am not mistaken, viruses also have similar features. They can't nourish or reproduce themselves alone, they need to live off a cell to develop. The egregora is a good analogy, a parasite of the mind, without its own life and possibility to develop.

Therefore many thought shapes are created and consequently, also really powerful egregora.

Every great energy such as a powerful egregora is capable of influencing many minds with maybe a dormant predisposition towards fanaticism which is suddenly reawakened by this huge energetic charge.

The strange thing about this is that the egregora, let's call it "in favour of abortion", is nurtured even by those who would resist with all their strength the absurd idea of killing a baby in the maternal womb.

The consequence is the emergence of an energetically powerful "thing", which by its nature, is not favourable to a correct and balanced development of man and is capable of creating conflict and social dislocation which, in the specific, result in the murder of abortionists.

The elections in Italy have brought to mind another shining example of the egregora.

The centre-right has just won the elections again, inflicting a heavy defeat on the left. How is this possible?

The premier of the centre-right and his party have a clear policy of self-interest and falsification, they have undergone a series of scandals that should have logically led them to certain defeat.

The opposition continuously and bitterly criticized him during and before the election campaign.

Yet the prize given to the centre-right by the electorate was evident.

As far as I can see, the discussion is quite clear.

A powerful egregora was formed, generated by distorted and emotionally absorbing thoughts by the government which were blown out of proportion by the opposition in a futile attempt, evident with hindsight, to oppose them.

In this case it is particularly interesting to observe how important the mass media was in amplifying this and how it became a fundamental tool for the growth of the egregora thanks to the involvement of the thoughts of millions of people.

Television in particular, is an extraordinary disseminator of egregore, thanks to its possibility of extensively conveying distorted thoughts and the emotions which are connected with them.

I would also say that television is an extraordinary tool in so far as it is "neutral".

It depends on the use that is made of it.

But if it is used as I have just described, television becomes a curse for the human race, a tool that allows the uncontrolled growth of regressive egregore.

Energetic dynamics.

I want to deepen the discussion on the formation of egregore at least a little bit more, because I believe that on our voyage to "true knowledge", it is fundamental to know that if there is a "sick" idea (or more generally, an "Evil" action), the idea which strongly opposes it, the supposedly "healthy" idea or the bearer of "Good", does nothing less than energetically nurture the egregora generated by the former.

With this type of dynamic, you do not escape from the problem.

You do not escape from the conflict or the illness, social or personal, or its consequences.

I know that this idea might sound absurd and in opposition to what you have thought or to what they have taught you, but it is what I was told by the Masters.

When we think about it, is this not just maybe what Christ meant with his famous "… turn the other cheek"?

We have always understood it to mean "avoiding violence with violence", but a deeper meaning could be to "avoid opposing Evil with its counterpart", because in doing so we do nothing less than play into its hands.

The solution to the problem is incredibly simple.

We have to stop thinking and struggling against that sick idea (… against Evil, if you like), because this is the only way of not nurturing it, from an energetic point of view.

In [14] I read *"you find yourself in a core nurtured by the wrath of human beings.*

It is only a balloon, which will deflate as soon as you stop fearing it, as soon as you stop struggling against it.

Stop resisting it, because by doing so, you confer it with reality. Recognize it for what it is: a mass of energy, which, if it is not nurtured, will disappear in the same way that it came.

It will disappear before your eyes and only act upon those who go on nurturing it".

As you may have guessed from the above, we have the possibility of "pulling out" from destructive dynamics or, better, those that are socially or personally regressive.

This discussion can begin to let us understand that there are mechanisms in our reality that are substantially energetic at the base of all of life's functions, be they material, psycho-social or spiritual.

You may say that this is the cold conclusion of an engineer, wholly devoted to the understanding of functioning mechanisms and who sees energy everywhere, but who has not got a heart beating in his breast.

I can assure you that this is not the case, and I can guarantee that if we do not understand that the "heart", like the thought, move energies, we will never reach "true knowledge", the only one that allows us to evolve.

The collective thought shapes are not only egregore.

From what has been said above, we can understand that egregore are the creations of collective thought, indeed, the thoughts of many individuals.

The effect is basically negative, that is to say that the egregora is considered to be the result of a distorted and "emotionalized" thought, if I can say so, which does not help the equilibrium or harmonic development of the human race.

However, there are other types of collective thought, e.g. ideologies.

They are a widespread thought that have a precise energy but a lesser emotive content than egregore.

An ideology can however become an egregora. It becomes so when it leads to conflict or war.

In such a case an ideology is "attacked" by the wrathful feelings of individuals who degenerate the basic idea of the ideology itself and adorn it with many single distorted and emotionally regressive thoughts.

At first, ideology is a strong thought endowed with its own energy as opposed to an egregora which lives from the union of many thoughts.

It represents a typology of collective thought that is potentially capable of giving rise to strong changes in the social environment, and as such, it is an evolutionary tool, not of an individual, but more of a whole community.

If it changes into an egregora it too becomes a regressive tool.

In its initial stage, ideology rises from a non-human base.

It comes, as it were, through a suggestion to a human representative from one or more spiritual entities who care for the development of man.

Apart from the suggestion in man's mind, the same entities help, through a series of "coincidences" that have nothing to do with chance, to make sure that the idea is widely spread and accepted by human beings.

The "diffusion" phase of the idea (ideology) is such that it is energetically self-nurturing, exploiting the energy of the thoughts of individual men, who lend themselves to accept it and personally carry it forward.

We have spoken about ideology, but there are other "strong collective thoughts" which are the spur to an evolution of the human race.

For example, strong scientific ideas.

These men of genius who have introduced them, are nothing more than human beings of a higher level who have been trusted with ideas which come from the Spirit.

At this point let's go back a few pages to the paragraph "The origin of great human discoveries".

Let's look again at how these "revolutionary" ideas are transmitted into the minds of those "pre-destined" men.

Talking about scientific ideas, at CERN in Geneva, they are trying to verify the existence of the boson of Higgs[63], also known as "the God particle".

Its possible experimental discovery could allow the confirmation of a new vision of what is the basis of things, which is not only relative to the scientific aspect of knowledge but involves a way in itself of conceiving existence and could possibly lead to important technological innovations and changes in the social environment.

It is a clear example of the overall evolution of human beings.

---

63   Higgs is the scientist who was the first to introduce the particle in question in one of his theories. The boson of Higgs is particular because it carries out a key role in the global theory of particles (standard model) and it is the only one in that environment that has not yet been detected experimentally. In the appendix I talk about some popular information on the subject. It is noted that even if the boson of Higgs' is a mistake, the idea that it might exist has generated a series of consequences that constitute an evolution in the process of knowledge.

But the experimental verification has nothing to do with the "discovery" of this particle.

Instead the idea of its existence came about when it was conceived in the mind of a scientist who, the Masters tell me, was not the eponymous Higgs.

Someone On High gave a little "nudge" to the man of "science" to further a new step in the evolution of the "understanding" on the part of human beings.

A completely analogous process comes from the art field.

The example of rock paintings[64] started by men some tens of thousands of years ago or the birth of an important new artistic movement which revolutionised the previous way of conceiving art.

I am thinking here about the introduction of perspective in painting or the Gothic style in architecture.

I would like to add that every great cultural movement, in the widest sense of the word, had similar origins, the Renaissance is an example.

Therefore the evolution of the human race came through "great ideas" of a non-human origin that were introduced to men to use to their advantage.

Understanding this is a hard blow to human pride, it was not man who gave the spur to his evolutionary phases.

However man can do a very important thing: he can favour these "evolutionary nudges" and not oppose them.

Aligning with these means aligning to evolution as he has been asked.

Generally, pride impedes this alignment.

Prides isolates man and makes him believe that he only has to rely on his own strengths.

This is not how it is.

The return to "true knowledge" is gradually demonstrating this to us.

---

64 Graham Hancock's tome "Shamans" [16], attributes "trips" under the effects of drugs as the first inspiration of humans to communicate graphically. In fact the altered state of consciousness provoked by the drugs allowed dimensions, not normally visible, to be reached and from which subsequently bring back "something" on returning to normality.

We cannot evolve in only one sphere.

From what we have seen, the introduction of new ideas to men and their subsequent spread favours the evolution of the human race in a certain sphere.

We must not think that evolution only happens in one sphere. Man must be able to advance in a complete way, precisely because we can talk about evolution.

Fortunately such a process comes about normally, when an advance is made in one field, e.g. science, it leads to parallel advances in other fields, which together can make man grow in his entirety.

An example could be that a discovery in science could lead to a subsequent technological application that would free man from excessive physical burdens and consequentially allow him to dedicate time to activity in the social field of benefit to other men and thus developing a general common well-being.

We can find lots of examples of this but ... the opposite is also the case.

There are cases in which great scientific discoveries have worsened the lives of a huge amount of people.

The discovery of nuclear fission comes to mind, on the one hand it contributed enormously to the growth of our understanding of the sub-atomic world with important and useful applications in the field of medicine for example.

On the other hand, it led to the atomic bomb and the consequent spread of much pain and fear among men.

Let's get to a very important conclusion immediately.

Innovative ideas are offered to us from On High, they can help us grow and we are also given a hand to extend them and their beneficial effect on humans.

However, these same ideas can be carried forward autonomously by man (a type of free will ...) who can either use them for good or degenerate them in the worst way.

And this is really where man's destiny comes into play.

Heaven has predisposed its growth in a certain direction, but man can choose to follow it or go elsewhere with who knows what consequences.

The greatest responsibility trusted to man comes into play, he can choose to evolve in the right direction or ... cease to exist because he chose the wrong one.

This is always where the "knowledge" factor intervenes.

Man, as well as being able to choose the direction to take, can simply choose the wrong one because he does not know the right one!

Correct knowledge, true knowledge is therefore the basis of man's choice.

And true knowledge does not come from man.

A *new concept of truth.*

Speaking of "true knowledge" immediately conceives the parallel with the concept of "truth".

In general, we men have a rather banal concept of truth. Something is true in our experience, if it can be verified in a certain way and continues to be verified in the same way. Something is true if it concurs with the "effective reality" which we experiment.

Paradoxically, it is a subjective concept, supported by our personal experimentation that is contemporaneously considered objective.

It almost brings me to say that such a concept of truth is closer to illusion, we consider to be true what seems true, and the word "illusion" is completely contained in that "seems".

In other words, a truth that is a little true and rather illusory!

We often use the word "truth" with a different meaning, in content it is ideally accepted as absolute and unquestionable, often from a religious point of view.

This definition is probably better than the first, but even this, all things considered, is quite illusory, indeed, in our perception maybe more illusory than the first because it lacks that impression of verifiability that the first is endowed with.

It also appears fragile faced with the "multitude" of different and opposite truths which various religions profess.

Therefore this definition seems illusory, ambiguous and less demonstrable than the first when faced with the "reality" we experiment in the material world.

The definition of what is the "truth" is a problem that has put many philosophers to the test, each one reaching their own conclusion, up to those, who have given up in the face of such complexity and concluded with the affirmation that the only plausible thing is to admit the existence of many truths, even with the contradictions between them.

Allow me to propose another concept of truth that the Masters suggested to me.

They tell me that there is only one great and absolute "Truth": The Creator.

There is only one absolute Truth because it has to be immutable, and only the Creator is endowed with this characteristic.

Instead, Creation is a continually mutable "existence" and as such cannot be endowed with absolute aspects.

The absolute Truth of Creation is therefore only the Creator[65] who, for his part[66], is above Creation itself.

Due to this fact, we, created beings, cannot access knowledge of the Creator until we are part of Creation[67,68], for the moment we have not been conceded the understanding of the only absolute Truth.

It is a Truth we are inclined towards but is not yet within our reach.

Therefore … it is useless that we should get worried about the only absolute Truth.

We have to content ourselves with the relative truths that belong to Creation; it is in this environment where all our commitment to "true knowledge" plays and to which all my books are substantially dedicated.

Now we have to try and reach a definition of "relative truth", which is the only type of truth with a direct application and benefit for us.

From now on I will mean "truth" by this.

The definition which was suggested to me is this: *it is truth which aligns*

---

65   In fact, Creation is part of the Creator and the Creator part of Creation.

66   To divide the Creator in parts is absurd, but it is the only way to let us appreciate this concept that is so far from our perception. In approximately correct terms we also have to say that that part of the Creator which is above Creation does not exist, supposing "existent" is only that which belongs to Creation.

67   Only when we return to the Creator at the end of the voyage of Creation, and therefore not be Creation anymore, we will be able to access this Knowledge.

68   I have discussed this unknowable aspect of the Creator in my third book [4] in relation to the interpretation of the Zodiac of Dendera.

us to the correct path that has to be fulfilled because we can, one day, come out from Creation and be reabsorbed in the absolute Truth.

In other words everything that allows us to go along the "Right Path" of the return to the Creator, is truth.

I am aware that this assertion can appear to be somewhat vague for our mental desire of clarity and objectivity, but it is the only "true" definition of "truth" that is possible.

A whole series of rather "nasty" consequences for our normal way of thinking, spring from this definition:

a. a unique truth does not exist for everyone, it is dependent on the path of every single being and of the "evolutionary" level they have reached;

b. truth becomes obligatorily "relative" and therefore we have to abandon the idea of an objective truth;

c. we have to abandon the idea that reason can suggest what truth is to us;

d. the truth is not something detectable by man, because his really restricted vision on the "path" is such that it impedes him from having a sufficiently broad view in order to establish what is true and what is not;

e. we have to, if we want to access the truth, obligatorily put our faith in Someone endowed with a "broad vision" and capable of informing us what is "truth" for us;

f. we must learn to pick up the information that this "Someone" is trying to send us in relation to "our" truth.

I am well aware that these statements could annoy many people, but this is the truth that was transmitted to me and it became "mine": in such a way as to spur me on to affirm it.

I well know that it is fastidious for all the official religions for whom relative truths cannot exist and that there is only "their truth"; if we think well about it, only the existence of different religions is a manifest demonstration of their relativity and, more so, of the relativity of the truths they present.

I also annoy all the ideologies and social organizations who make their own way of conceiving human development as an absolute and generate conflict with those who think differently.

I get under the skin of all of those spiritual organizations, sects and parties who want to conceive a unique scenario of human development and progress.

Let us forget the man of science, still convinced that rationality and objectivity are not only precious tools of knowledge of the material world, which they are, but that they are "absolutes" capable of explaining all of "Creation".

"My" relative truth, in synthesis, hurts the sensitivity of a proud man who thinks he can make it alone and does not understand being part of a whole much bigger than him and endowed with thousands of different roads of development, all of them true.

A new concept of the relationship between good and evil.

In the sphere of true knowledge, between relative and "personalized" truths that I spoke about, it is still possible to identify sufficiently general and "true" dynamics to establish guidelines that can be applied, for example, to the human race in its wholeness.

The latter are a type of "universal principles" of the dynamics of Creation as a whole, and it is correct to keep to them if we want to be and stay on the "Right Path".

They were introduced and described in human history by great characters: Jesus comes to mind, but going back in time I see Thoth[69], the Egyptian God, and his Emissaries, the main "introducers".

There is one of these dynamics that I want to talk about, because it is unacknowledged among the "universal principles" that are normally found in the texts which put them forward.

Therefore, I want to speak about the dynamics of the relationship between good and evil.

What do we normally mean by good and evil?

In general, good is seen as something which corresponds to usefulness, advantage, a positive condition.

"Good", in substance, something useful, is an extremely vague term, it is a poorly defined and indefinable concept.

---

69   In my third book [4] I remember that Thoth (or Tehut, the correct Egyptian name) was the universal Demiurge (the Creator even), the God who brought the work of creation to an end *by only the sound of his voice* [26].

With this simple statement one can already understand the extreme relativity of the concept of good i.e. what is good for you, might not be good for me.

In the sphere of relative good we often manage to perceive an absolute Good, but even that is rather "variable" in the idea we have of it in our heads.

For some, absolute Good is what maximizes their own personal advantage, others connect it to their country, others to an ideology, others to a religion and still others to God.

... I would say that there is a lot of confusion on what is good or Good.

Vice versa, evil is seen as something which constitutes a reason of detriment in the face of a certain convenience, then arriving at absolute Evil seen as the "Principle" of negation and destruction and often portrayed by diabolical figures.

Here again, the same can be said about evil as was said about good, difficult to define and relative to the concept.

To sum up, we can say that good and evil are two very general and personal concepts of advantage and disadvantage with the net sensation that everything that is evil should be opposed with all our strength and destroyed and eliminated in some way.

As a matter of fact, many people dedicate their lives to the triumph of good and the destruction of evil.

In an attempt to understand more, let us now see what the Masters told me.

Above all, They made it clear that the concept of good cannot exist without the concept of evil, in other words if we destroy evil we also destroy good.

When I had the chance to ask [2] the Masters if it would be appropriate to renounce Evil, They answered me:

> "We must never renounce Evil, given that it leads us to
> Good. Tabling such a discussion to exclude any kind of
> evil, turns against us and aggravates the situations.
> The evil prosecuted + or -.

Good and Evil collaborate in the creation but
it is not due to being liked by man.
They are in a relationship as the "we have" and the "we are":

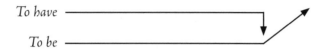

To have

To be

The resolution is conception of extreme Evil.
The idea is from God. To man, the work".

At that time I interpreted their answer as an affirmation that both Good and Evil are necessary and integral parts of Creation, and are collaborating elements of it.

Evil is a tool that leads us to Good, and to exclude Evil (or evil) in general does not help us, indeed it worsens our situation.

Evil can act on us in an obvious or less obvious way, with the consequence of a greater or lesser desire to eliminate it.

Good and evil are both active agents in the Creation … which has little interest in whether it pleases us or not.

That's the way it is.

Both are tools that take part in the evolution of Creation and as long as there is Creation they will exist.

Thinking of destroying evil/Evil (or good /Good) is a useless human fantasy.

They illustrated the action mechanism of Good/Evil to me by likening it to one of Having/Being in which the parallel path (in the path of evolution be it the single soul, or more generally, that of the human race) at a certain point leads to the fall of "having" and the rise of "being".

In this analogy there is not a direct parallelism between having-evil and being-good, it is meant only to say that at a certain point, one of the two entities will prevail without cancelling out the other.

And while there is a "Divine" trend on the overall outcome of Creation[70],

---

70 What will happen has already been established, it is just that we human beings do not know how it will be. We like to think that it will be "Good" which will triumph at the "end of time", but in fact, we do not know.

within its single "sub-systems"[71] there is the possibility that the outcome could be of one type or the other, good could prevail over evil or vice versa.

This is a very important aspect of the discussion because it tells us, a priori, that our single system (ourselves, for example, or the human race as a whole) is not inevitably aligned to the general destiny of Creation.

A determining role is played by what is known as a "free will" or better, our personal (but also as humans, or the planet ...) choice of taking one direction or another.

This is where the "true knowledge" that we have been talking about comes into play.

And it is always here where the help and stimulus that other non-physical beings (e.g. the Masters, and also those who are not necessarily on the side of good) try to give us, also comes into play.

The Masters suggested that in the prevalence of good over evil, without any of the two disappearing until the end of time, the passage onto the next step of evolution plays: if we as single souls or the human race as a whole "lean" towards good, then our "promotion" to the next phase of development becomes probable or better, we continue to live moving in the direction of evolutive progress.

The opposite is the case if we are routed on an involutional path that will probably lead to our final disappearance from Creation.

Note well that I always speak about "leaning" towards good, never about a decisive direction towards it.

An excessive direction towards good exposes us to a powerful re-entry of evil, with the destruction of a type of equilibrium only slightly oriented to good which should gradually lead us towards evolution, be it personal, as the human race, as a planet.

Allow me to make a scholastic comparison, we must aim for a bare pass, a poor 51 out of 100 in favour of good ... anyone who wants to go for absolute excellence, 100%, is exposed to the risk of a nervous breakdown that could set them back a year, or their jealous classmates could beat them up so that they end up in hospital and the consequent loss of an academic year, or in the worst case, life.

---

71 For example, a human soul is a single system, as is also the human race or the planet Earth or an extraterrestrial people.

It is the same as saying an exaggerated good exposes us to the re-entry of an exaggerated evil: from 100% we can suddenly drop down to zero.

In general, religions push towards an exaggerated good, failing to understand the mechanism I have just tried to describe.

Only some of them have grasped it, Buddhism comes to mind when it says that we have to "walk on the razor's edge".

In other words, the position we have to take is to incline towards being on the thinnest of blades which divides good on one side, and evil on the other.

The imbalance which comes from leaning decisively and uniquely towards good, generates for example, fanaticism which is widespread in not only the religious field.

Good and evil therefore have to exist and run almost parallel existences until the moment the "exams" come around when a slight lean towards good will allow us to reach pass marks and be promoted to the next stage of evolution.

If we fail one year, it does not mean that we cannot re-sit the year and complete the scholastic cycle, even if a bit late.

However, if we fail two or three times in a row ... we will have to break with our studies and leave the school of evolution.

Let's go back to the phrase of the Masters I talked about above, it is completed by stating that that mechanism of parallelism of good/evil, with a slight prevalence of one over the other, in determined moments, is broken at a certain point and this comes about when we reach the "conception of an extreme Evil".

The concept of an extreme Evil only exists beyond Creation, an environment where we can only "stutter" the existence[72] of an absolute Good or an absolute Evil that no longer run parallel or interact with each other.

For the moment that environment is too far from the possibility of our perception and as such, is of no investigation or use.

The Masters concluded by reaffirming that the idea of a good-evil mechanism is Divine, man's duty is only to live with this mechanism, even if he does not like it.

I tried to investigate the above argument further on another occasion[73]

---

72 Do you think it is possible to say "exist" outside of Creation?
73 You can find the original of this disquisition in [2].

by asking the Masters if they could tell me how evil and good co-exist and how they confront and combat one another.

Seeing the importance of the argument, the Masters chose a different way of answering from the usual, that is through "connection" in which A[74] left space for the Master who spoke directly through her. Her voice was recorded with a digital recorder and then I transcribed the content.

I have wholly written everything said in that connection, seeing the beauty and the depth that was transmitted to me.

"The answer, as you already know, follows the rhythm of previous answers on various subjects and goes towards the aim of Truth.
If, at first, a person says I am sick, I am better or I am fine, by this he is indicating a state of health seen in a very self-centred way. Given that his being better, being fine or being sick highlights a displacement of the arguments in other people, because for them, being better, being fine or being sick borders on another truth, everyone has their own.
Being better for a person who has suffered a serious road accident could mean being up to his neck in plaster but still alive.
Therefore the truth for everyone follows a line of discussion that is too personalized to reach a definition of good and evil in its original sense.
In the original sense both good and evil did not co-exist in the same person. To co-exist can mean having weak arms and strong legs or vice versa.
Therefore under the sign of the authority of good and evil.
And so, in the original sense, the coexistence was not preselected, predicted or foreseen.
Man's, human being's exaggeration of food and wine was particularly important in the next stage.
This exaggeration enabled the introduction of evil, i.e. the state of drunkenness, what was seen as good before, a half glass of wine. The same exaggeration, that was better defined as a good appetite, a solid hunger but without excess of food, at the beginning, later became indigestion.
Therefore good and evil did not co-exist together at the origin.

---

74   Re-read who A is in the introduction.

Thanks to the mistakes[75] the one above being a banal example, the unity of good and evil was re-awakened, unity in the sense of "in a unique circle", where good and evil tie and pull together and you wonder how far good leads to evil in the sense that a "carafe of wine, an abundant plate of food can run the risk of a debt to Heaven through the state of drunkenness and indigestion" up to the point where the illness of indigestion and drunkenness can reawaken the attention of man's awareness to return to the original equilibrium in food and drink. Therefore, ended the original state, thanks to man's mistake, it becomes a state in two, united in a single circle, so co-existence becomes possible. And the sign of Tao is established[76] that is to say, two opposite directions of an abyssal difference, but held together by the same circle, which does not cure the individual, indeed it always squeezes him more. Until it becomes a tiny hole through which pass, like the slot in a lock, to cross over, reaching the stage of death. Because in error man continues, despite everything, to grow reducing himself until he passes to the other side and, in his arrival phase, becomes a minuscule point which reaches the other side under the shape of a megalithic disc in error. The tolerance in error is minimal[77] but good and evil are conceived and united in the error, in the same circle.

---

75 In fact man is not the only being of Creation to have made this "mistake". There are other "peoples" and systems of Creation who live in the same situation. For the moment if we manage to understand our own situation that will be a lot… leave the others to move themselves.

76 The sign of Tao has a wider meaning than only the mechanism of good and evil which we are talking about, but it is useful because it illustrates very well how two diverse entities like Ying and Yang can be contained in a unique circle. Both penetrate, mix and enclose each other but at the same time remain separate in their basic essence; it is also significant that there is an almost total equilibrium between the two, highlighted by their identical shapes and dimensions.

77 The part highlighted does not lend itself to an immediate understanding; I will try to re-write it in my own words. In the moment in which the unitary and original state ends following man's mistake, a dual state is born where good and evil can co-exist in a single environment and establish the sign of Tao, or better, the fact that two elements separated by an abyss are held together and forced to remain inside a circle (a defined environment); and such an environment does not help man to be cured of his "mistake", indeed, it makes him fall even lower. This "fall" is represented by the circle which always shrinks around man until it

*Therefore the growth phase of man has built this possibility. In origin the
intervention was double sided, obviously everything for good or for evil.
There was not a middle road.
There was not co-existence in a unique circle.
Man's tolerance[78] did not allow this and urged the calling
of good and evil to co-exist on the same platform.
The human mind conceived this mistake and therefore takes on
the responsibility of laying good and evil in a unique circle."*

We therefore understand from the above that originally good and evil
were two separate entities, in fact, as the Masters told me,

"two adverse solutions".

Which means that

*"they were like two fluids, from currents which directed things
in a way that they never conflicted but both lived in high or
low spheres without coming across any difficulty".*

They achieved, in substance, a

*"stage of autonomous relationship without any type of discord; there
was nothing conflicting between them, between the two of them".*

becomes so small that it is comparable with a miniscule hole through which one
can "pass" as if it were a hole in a lock which allows the door to be opened and to
go on through. This "go on through" means to die a non-physical death, the death
of "error", or the exit from this circle where good and evil co-exist and the return
to the original unitary state. In the "error" however, man, despite everything,
continues to grow and evolve, erring less, in a continuous process until he passes
through, and when he is ready to pass through, he becomes like the tiniest of dots
which passing through is transformed into a massive boulder capable of smashing
and completely demolishing the error. Tolerance, i.e. the ability to withstand
without suffering damage what is or can be dangerous in this "circle" of error, is
minimal but ...

78 Here tolerance is understood differently from what was considered a few lines
above; here it substantially means "the level of understanding".

Man's error[79], due to his initial lack of understanding of Creation's mechanism (or more so, to being insufficiently evolved), has virtually united good and evil in a single environment and their two "currents" began to interact frenetically, mixing like two different coloured liquids into a single fluid, but still internally maintaining their distinct colours.

By law of "homogenization", if there is too much of one type of colour, the opposite colour immediately acts to re-establish a type of "optimal blend" characteristic of our state.

In other words, this is the meaning of the Buddhist request to "walk on the razor's edge"; maintaining a perfect equilibrium, an optimal blend between good and evil.

Egypt springs to mind here, in my third book [4], speaking about the Zodiac of Dendera, I rediscovered the representation of the god Anubf with a star, this symbolizes that he was an "elect from Heaven", a Messiah.

One intermediate attribute of His represented two beings who, as much as they seemed like animals with a circlet on their heads, are in fact two entities of the spirit.

This indicates that Anubf was a person made up of two "spiritual" entities contemporaneously present in the same physical body.

This aspect makes Anubf an especially particular god; of the two spirits of which he was comprised one was good and one was evil.

Only by having both in him could he understand the correct equilibrium between these two great forces which activate the game of life, not only in the material sphere.

The aim of Anubf was not to make one triumph over the other but simply to maintain both in the right relationship, be it in matter or spirit.

Anubf was a very powerful character, he worked to re-equilibrate the rapport between good and evil.

---

79 In fact, it is not really a man's "error", but it was Creation itself which had introduced this mechanism, by inserting in itself, beings, who not knowing the "Truth", through the mechanism of "error" and "false interpretation" were forced to gradually understand and correct themselves in order to return to the Truth. Maybe it is banal to say so ... but the sense of man and his evolution is substantially a path of knowledge to make him come out of the mistaken interpretation of Reality. This is what is wanted by the Creator! But do not ask me why.

Good and evil in equilibrium in any case.

That is the way it is, even if we are not used to seeing the relationship between good and evil like this.

But, there is more.

Given that it is the human mind that makes the mistake, "*it also leads human beings to think less well and or act less well, but the direction*", beyond human error, "*is to get well being back* or, better, *being in the Light*".

In simple terms, when man manages to come out from his mistake, good and evil will separate into two currents which are no longer inter-active and man will find himself in one of the two ... some men in good and some in evil!

The Masters who suggest what I am writing mean to help me and as many men as possible to get the "good" current back.

In this sense they are using me to transmit a "true knowledge" which allows me and us to come out from the "error".

"*... and thus complying with this principle, human beings become the Light again, which they were in origin and from there they no longer move in the sense "in the Light they are found and in the light they remain". In fact, that is the separation[80]. At the end of reincarnations there will be a real cut off between Good and Evil, when the soul has retrieved everything with the aim of being in the Light, of entering into the Light and Evil no longer intervenes*".

The path of our soul[81], passing through more reincarnations, is really made to gradually be able to understand the error which we have fallen into.

When we have completed it, it will no longer be necessary to reincarnate and our soul will be able to "cut" the mixture of good and evil; if we have managed to re-enter into the Light[82], Evil will no longer have anything to do with us.

---

80 The separation from the Light is really constituted by the "fall" into error, this is the real meaning of the "original sin" of Christians.

81 **N.B.: it is a path of the single soul, not of the entire human race! The single soul could also continue to develop and "understand the error" in environs different from the terrestrial.**

82 But we might not manage it ...

How to "use" good and evil.

In the course of various discussions with the Masters, different and even "trivial" considerations emerged on how best to use and understand the good-evil mechanism which I have tried to describe above.

For example, on the question if good and evil represent a duality like hot/cold or others from the physical world, I was answered that there are some dualities just from the physical world and limited to it.

Good and evil are in the physical world (the body) and also beyond it (the spirit), it is of a high nature and a deep meaning.

Asking if evil can be annulled, they said that:

> *"energy is + and –.*
> *If you are a Saint it is thanks to Evil".*

Just as electrical current needs two different inter-connected polarities to generate its movement, good and evil are the two poles that generate an "energetic" transfer; one cannot exist without the other.

The idea of an extreme good, Sanctity, is only conceivable thanks to the existence of evil.

Therefore, good and evil represent an indispensable dualism. They told me:

> *"Duality is resonance of the One".*

By which it is meant that the One resonates in duality, namely that duality is the possibility of the One to highlight and amplify itself.

For us it is the possibility we are given to understand the One.

There is no movement without duality, there is no understanding and no evolution.

Good and evil are a necessary and indispensable expression of duality. We may as well "exploit" it as best we can!

It follows that it is useless to fight and wish to defeat and annul evil, it also is part of God.

"It is better to use its symbols and sometimes accept its dross, but only to reduce its range and above all increase its humiliation."

Evil is therefore not fought, indeed, it is exploited in some way, accepting the consequences.

All of this is to reduce its range and influence at levels balanced with good.

Evil has to be humiliated.

Evil has to be "deluded" but not beaten.

The attempts of excess which evil tends to and which always differentiates it from good have to be repulsed, and it will be made to understand that it cannot go beyond a certain level ... but it must never be defeated.

During the long periods passed together with A and B, the Master gave me a lot of information and indications about my personal development and many of them were regarding the behaviour to have towards evil.

During a certain phase, when I was being taught to become an energetic therapist, during therapy they highlighted the necessity to shield myself from being harmed by "dirty" or "malign" energy that I might absorb from people I was treating or receive in moments in which one is especially open and vulnerable, due to the specific condition in which you have to be to work correctly.

In such contexts They advised me, among other possible techniques, to utilize an extreme decision, almost a controlled "anger", against evil; this increases the energy and constitutes a natural screen.

A good screening effect is also given from working in pairs.

For example A told me that the work done with B was extremely important.

The fact of working in two constitutes a type of protection against Evil, because in general, you are more exposed to its influence when you undertake a rapid path of evolution by yourself similar to the one I was trying to do.

When there are two of you, Evil does not go directly to the single person but is "undecided" between going to one or the other and "wavers" without being very effective.

On another occasion I asked Them if I should take part in a course where energetic therapists, with the help of the Masters of light, were teaching how to clean up the various types of energetic "dirt", my Masters strongly advised me not to participate.

The justification for such advise rested in the fact that those therapists did not have sufficient knowledge of evil and could not adequately pass on to people who disinfest, what they actually know how to do, how to be careful after cleaning, of the incursion of new unwanted contaminations.

The cleaning up makes the subject more visible to unwanted incursions, especially evil ones and therefore the situation that follows could be worse than before.

They told me that there was no real advantage attending these courses, many of them promise the moon and the stars but the teachers neither know nor put in the right light the good-evil dynamics present in life.

Another dark aspect of these courses, or of all people obsessed with the afterlife, too fixed on the spiritual and too little on the material, is that they are easily subject to the temptation of pride (they think they are superior) which is an instrument of evil and they do not recognize the importance of physical life and they cannot exploit it for their evolution.

They are not able to understand that experience that allows us to evolve is made and found in matter and has to be lived to the full, recognizing its importance and sacredness.

Going back to the course on energetic cleaning, the Masters emphasized, in particular, that before carrying out that type of cleaning on people, it is much more important to teach them "cerebral transmission", or in other words, let them understand how to send the right messages through the brain or better, the "mind".

In essence it is fundamental, to re-programme, through the conscious use of thought, certain mental behaviours that cause the attraction of specific types of "evil" or "negative energy" if you prefer.

I have a clear example of this mechanism at hand.

A patient of A and B, who I studied for a series of sittings over a number of years, demonstrated in herself, in the first analysis that I carried out, the presence of numerous energetic "parasites"[83], thought shapes[84] and, at a certain point also a disembodied soul[85].

After a period of treatment from A and B, the presence of these energetic "annoyances" had completely disappeared.

At the same time A and B worked hard to eliminate what is called in technical terms "negative programming", in other words, a person's way of thinking that continuously goes against their "well-being", specifically, we are talking about an accentuated form of pride[86].

A and B did not manage to eliminate this negative programming, and they decided to interrupt the treatment at a certain point given its uselessness.

Some time ago, a little over a year after that interruption, I re-examined the person and I noticed the re-acquisition both of some parasites and of the disembodied soul.

The situation was not "serious" like it had been before the cure but it was worsening little by little, if the negative programming was not modified or if the person did not change her way of thinking, the gradual accumulation of these "negative energetic factors" would make her mental and physical state worse than what it was before the cleaning.

This is like saying that a lot of work had been done for nothing, indeed, her pre-existent state had worsened.

And the Masters do not like "working" without getting results!

Another interesting aspect of my "education" of this period linked in some way to the good/evil relationship, was the analysis of some of the activities I had carried out in previous lives.

---

83 By "parasites" I mean energetic agglomerates that are more or less big and annoying, which can nest in some part of the body and remain there for years. In general they constitute an energetic disturbance for the person, they impoverish him/her energetically and, in the long term, they can generate physical illness. Their origin is due to a trauma of either a physical or psychological type.

84 We have already seen what thought shapes are (see chapter "thought shapes, agents of illness"); I only want to repeat their "mental" origins here, that is to say, the fact that they are generated by our thoughts.

85 I have briefly dealt with the discussion about disembodied souls that can establish themselves in the body of a living person in my first book [2]; you can find a more detailed analysis in [21].

86 I talk about how harmful pride is in the chapter "the voyage".

It came out, for example, that I had been an exorcist at a high level, I had carefully avoided putting myself in the most difficult situations and I preferred to identify new techniques and pass them on to others.

This activity allowed me, in some way, to acquire good skill in dividing good from evil, a skill that I still have.

Quite often I feel sorry that others also do not have this possibility of "sub-division" and who strive on things that harm them, while it seems so clear to me what one is and what the other is.

A completely personal aspect of this came out when I asked the Master if I would be asked to be an exorcist again in this life, He answered me:

> *"it is your karma to be an exorcist for 1/3, with the skill to "pull yourself away from + serious cases just in time", for another third your karma is the "availability that grows instead towards diagnosis, identification", the last third is that there are "people who are around you charged with the pleasure of annoying you"."*

So my karma is not "fully" that to re-become an exorcist, I will have the occasion to be one even if I manage to avoid the most serious cases that could over expose me to the conflict with evil.

In part, I have the skill to grow in the identification of illnesses and possessions.

However, I also have a certain "tendency" to attract people to me who are a little "perturbed" with the excuse that they want to be cured but instead only simply want to annoy me.

This is also an effect of the "balancing" of good/evil, but it should not create many problems for me if I am conscious of it and I face it the right way.

As you can see … it is not by chance that I dwell so much on the relationship between good and evil, I am up to my neck in it!

But do not make the mistake of thinking this has nothing to do with you, you are also fully involved in this mechanism, whether you like it or not.

I learned another interesting "technical" aspect in the treatment of the good/evil relationship during an investigation of some "shamanic" techniques[87], like the "voyage" that I described at the beginning of this book.

In these "voyages" one is particularly vulnerable during contact with entities from the most varied species and levels, some can be in one way or another "negative", or even "malignant".

Therefore it is especially important to be on your guard.

They told me that during these "voyages" the rational mind should never be completely excluded but that a part of it should always be working, let's say at least 10 or 15 per cent.

The mind is kept active in its role of "intellectual diffidence", in other words, in one way or another you have to keep your "feet on the ground" when you exaggerate with the "flight" so as to make you notice any "excessive deviations" that may occur.

It has to help us to "let go" if it notices that what we are facing is too dangerous or superior to our abilities.

It has to help us, at the level of method, to "betray" and cheat evil in order not to be betrayed by it.

Yes: evil is cheated by intelligence and decisiveness!

And the mind has to help us do it.

Another particular moment for the transmission and entrance in activity of evil is, listen, listen, when we make love.

I should say when we have sex, which is much less than making love.

Many people tend to lose themselves in sex, in this potentially splendid moment, forgetting their own individuality.

This behaviour temporarily brings down some of our energetic guards which we normally have and which protects us from aggression and the entrance of external "energetic agents".

It can therefore become a moment of great vulnerability, especially if

---

87   The Masters do not like talking much about "shamans". They say that they learn to use some entities present in dimensions beyond ours, and to operate transfers between the various dimensions, but they almost never have a broadened "vision" of what they are doing and they often activate a forcing that goes against the correct development of things. They once told me "*black magic is the illness, white magic is the convalescence, abstention is health*". The concept of magic is almost always associated with the "forcing of natural events" which should, instead, follow their own road.

our partner is not "energetically" clean, and decides, right at that moment, to discharge some of their refuse.

I know it is not very "romantic", but it is my duty to tell you that having sex "passively", completely forgetting yourselves in that marvellous moment of orgasm ... runs a risk that is not trivial.

I certainly do not want to tell you not have sex ... in fact the opposite!

But it is important that you do it a certain way.

It is absolutely necessary that during sex you remember to remain in yourselves, you must not lose yourself in the other person forgetting your own individuality.

To lose yourself means also to stop, or "become passive", this an equivalent form of saying we forget ourselves.

Some time ago, B explained to me that ideal conditions for the activities of evil and the transmission of energetic parasites between partners are created in sexual relationships, something that was later confirmed by the Masters.

The parasites nest especially in the coccyx[88], these are the ones that are most easily transmittable.

In this sense one should know the "energetic" past of your partner, something that is not easy for most people, and if they have parasites, or worse still, if they have been possessed.

I cannot dare to imagine what prostitutes get (B told me almost all of them have severe energetic problems, and he has cured many of them) and vice versa so have their clients.

... it seems like a great reason for carefully choosing your partner and avoiding uncontrolled and irresponsible sex.

I repeat that the last thing I want is to advise you to avoid sex, if it is done well it is a beautiful and important (for some fundamental) element of growth and evolution.

The Masters even defined it to me as

"the glory of love",

---

88 They are among the "toughest" that can be found in the body. Disembodied souls like the same particular area of the body. Furthermore, the coccyx zone is directly linked to the sexual organs.

but only if done the right way.

Otherwise it is a most effective instrument of the action of evil.

Talking about another angle of the good/evil relationship, an aspect that was highlighted to me is rather significant: examining patients affected by degenerative illnesses that are currently incurable such as multiple sclerosis and Parkinson's.

When a "rational" approach to one of these illnesses was tried by me or the patient, at a certain point I was given this answer:

"the rationalization of the experience of such an
illness does not contain solutions.
Beyond the reason of an illness there is a feast of evil".

They meant that an incurable degenerative illness of that type cannot be faced with reason, in the sense that it cannot be resolved with it.

When we face an incurable illness only with reason, it can only lead us to depression or to throw in the towel because of the lack of solutions or ways out and with such an outcome "evil is feasting" because it has achieved its objectives: desperation, abandonment, complete negativity.

Never lay down and give it the victory ... but that goes beyond reason.

Medical science cannot face up to this aspect; in fact its essentially rational methods play evil's game.

Medicine in its most widespread and officially recognized form has an important role in the creation of fear.

When it does not know something or how to cure an illness, it establishes the incurability of the illness in front of the patient (or relatives which is almost the same), generating discomfort and the "fear" of death.

Now then, the fear of death is one of the most "powerful"[89] fears we have and, in general, fear can be considered as an instruments of evil.

From an energetic point of view fear generates "energetic holes" in our aura through which "anything" can enter.

Therefore, in general, being scared means collaborating with evil in the sense of giving it free access to us.

When evil enters in us we strongly come out of the good/evil equilibrium

---

89 Fear of death is almost always the first to be responsible for lung cancer.

which I spoke at length about some pages earlier: if we cannot re-establish a balance we are led to physical death (illness[90] always gets worse) and, something much more important, we distance ourselves from the correct and balanced direction that our soul has asked us to follow in this life: in substance ... we waste this[91] earthly existence.

Still talking about the "training" I got regarding the energetic treatment of sufferers from illness or energetic deficiencies, I was taught the importance of adopting techniques to limit or block the influence of evil during treatment.

For example, the important use of thought was highlighted to me in these circumstances:

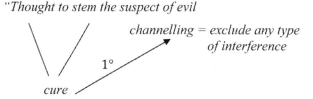

"Thought to stem the suspect of evil

channelling = exclude any type
of interference

1°

cure

to cure with thought set excludes
giving (leaving) space to evil;
do not give it your mental direction".

With the above they meant to tell me that thought is utilized to try to stem or put a barrier around the suspects and the ideas that Evil has about our work.

This is done by not letting it understand what our intentions are specifically in relation to the cure we aim to carry out.

During this type of energetic treatment, it becomes fundamental to "channel" or to carry out a direct transmission of the energetic input from

---

90 Illness is not only a consequence of fear: the energetic mechanism it generates is much more complex and articulated, but fear is an important vehicle of transfer, a type of energetic "infector".

91 Naturally, all is not lost. We can re-do it in some other subsequent life, even if we have slowed our evolution down by not correctly profiting from the chance given to us. If we slow down too much and miss too many chances ... we miss the train!

High that passes through us, and make it arrive in the most direct way possible to the person treated.

The fundamental thing of "channelling" is the fact of excluding any type of interference whatsoever, be it the "channeller's" mental interference or those due to "external agents" (I guarantee you that they can be innumerable).

Therefore in the energetic cure the first and most basic thing to do is to not undergo any interference; especially in the cure with thought set[92], the possibility of interference from evil must be excluded.

To do the above, first of all it is important that evil does not know the direction of our thought set direction, for example, if I absolutely want to cure someone and I go to him with a precise aim and already identified treatment, evil knows already what I intend to do and can try to block me in a thousand ways.

Instead, if I simply think about "going to see a friend", "maybe I'll treat him maybe not", that "the result will be whatever it will be, it's not that important" … evil will not know my thought set direction and/or will judge it to be of little importance for its aims and will not try to obstruct me.

Clearly, this does not exclude that evil can intervene later, during the treatment of the person involved, but at that point other mechanisms and "protection of the channelling" techniques come into play.

I am risking going too deeply into the specific here and it is best to close the discussion.

The good/evil dynamic has a particularly active role during sleep.

As I have already said, during sleep, we are in a distinct state in which the controls of our mind "loosen" and we are more pre-disposed compared to our awakened state, to contact with entities of various types from non-physical dimensions, some of whom are from the side of evil.

It is not rare for normally serene people to be badly disturbed by nightmares during the night.

This also happens because evil needs some "satisfaction" which it takes at night through nightmares and annoying dreams.

---

92 An energetic treatment is inextricably connected to the thought set of the person who follows it. It is the thought which links, activates and manages the energies that come into play during the channelling.

It is a little "forfeit" that we pay it when it does not manage to disturb us during the day, when our day runs smoothly.

In some way, this also helps that "walk on the razor's edge" dear to Buddhist tradition: it allows us to maintain a certain equilibrium in the good/evil relationship.

However, nights full of nightmares or traumatizing dreams say a lot about the exaggerated influence evil has on us during sleep and it is very probable the same influence also haunts us when we are awake, making life difficult for us.

We have said quite enough on the good/evil relationship.

Now, I would like to tell you about something about what is probably the most interesting topic for human beings, love.

Love.

Are we sure we know what love is?

Without doubt love is the subject most present in the lives of all of us; it is the most interesting, the most discussed, the most misunderstood, the least defined; it is that which involves us the most, which excites and disappoints; it is our engine and most of us could not imagine a life without it, and rightly so.

But, do we really know what it is?

Is it one "thing" or many different "things"?

I would like to make a parallel, which might seem a little heavy, but I believe that it renders the idea well.

In physics there are at least four defined types of force or better, interactions: electromagnetic, gravitational, weak and strong.

I do not want to go too deep with the argument[93] and tell you what they are, I simply want to highlight that scientists from all over the world have been searching "desperately" for years to find a theory that combines all these four inter-actions in a single complete framework that includes everything and is consistent.

The achievement of this objective has an almost divine "taste": it would allow us to say that "we men have finally understood how the universe functions": we have understood the unifying principle.

---

93 The aforementioned text by Lederman [19] allows you to further investigate the question.

But that research is revealing a kind of chimera … we could define it as the "Holy Grail" of physics [19].

Well, I believe that trying to define what love is, identifying its deep unity, is more or less the same thing: a chimerical unattainable research; but I will not give in a priori.

Even since antiquity, there has never been unity in defining love.

Many "relative" loves have always been contrasted to an absolute love (God?)[94], classically they were broken down into *agàpe* (αγάπη), unconditional and divine love; *philia* (φιλία) the love of affection and pleasure, from which a return is expected, as we do with friends; *eros* (ἔρως), sexual love.

Still more, there is *storge* (στοργή), the love of being part of something such as family ties, or even *thelema* (θέλημα) the pleasure of doing something, the desire of wanting to do …

We could spend days listing the various types of love, its sub-divisions, its variations, the different ways of interpreting its variations; it is almost a never ending discussion!

And what would you not do for the sake of love!

Let us say that it can take us from a sublime ecstatic joy to the gloomiest depths of depression; it can exalt us but also make us suffer; it spurs us to act in ways that are well beyond any reasonable type of behaviour and it pushes us to follow an idea that we love with all our strength.

It allows us to give and receive unimaginable tenderness but can push us to kill!

In general we associate it with something beautiful and desirable, but what is to be said when, for example, a girl kills herself for love?

How is it that it is always love?

I would like to stand apart from all these labels, sub-divisions and disquisitions that are basically created by man to interpret and define a part of reality in which he finds himself, and to fix on something which unites all these "separations" that are interpretive on what is the subject of love.

I would like to find something much more defined, if possible, but in any case transmitted by a much vaster Wisdom, that of the Masters.

I will go back to see what They told me in the past about the subject.

---

94   "God is love, and who remains in love, remains in God and God remains in him" (I John IV, XVI) [26,1].

I basically associated love with good, or a least something that tended towards good; but I was told:

*" love gives and takes or takes and gives and therefore we
find the same dynamic between good and evil".*

On the basis of the discussion above regarding the relationship between good and evil, I began to understand, above all, that love is neither good nor bad.

It is something else, however it has a dynamic that is similar to the good/evil relationship and is therefore endowed with a dual aspect.

The above quoted answer of the Masters was followed by this:

*"If the One exists, He needs union and the only One is Him where there
is good and evil and not ultra sensitivity and we will realize less well
if we do not understand Who is there to tell you and to give you".*

At first I did not understand the reason for that answer, it seemed like a change of argument, then I understood that to make sense of what love is, first of all one needs to perceive the existence of the One.

If we do that, it becomes more immediate to us, if you like, more logical, the fact that He requires union, or better, that everything must converge in Him, including good and evil which act on the Earth, love, and not only things which go beyond normal human sensitivity.

If we do not understand Who is "on high" and Who "tells" us, or better, Who allows us to understand the true sense of things, and Who "gives" us, or better, Who gives us the possibility of existence, we will achieve less on Earth.

This means that growth, or more so, the achievement of things on Earth, implies the perception of the One, or better, a religiosity of living.

Religion is not important.

Any of them can do.

But the religiosity of life is, it is fundamental!

Anyway, we have already reached an important conclusion: we cannot understand what love is if we do not have a "religiosity of living".

If we are in this state, we are already in a condition of perceiving that love has a dual nature which must be reunited in the One.

This is still somewhat "foggy", but something is beginning to unfold.

Then I was told:

"suffering is born from love and at times it kills".

Therefore, love that is generally seen as something good, something positive, is a "principle" which can also cause suffering and death, things which are normally considered bad or at least, negative.

Basically it seems that love is a counter-position (a duality) that generates movement, but also a priori closes in itself the necessity of a definite and definitive prevalence.

We have seen that, in a normal equilibrium between good and evil, an evolutionary mechanism is created which allows good to prevail only in the end.

What happens for love is analogous to the above, something that has to be maintained in life on Earth, to the detriment of the balance between its negative and positive aspects, and that at the end of our evolution can bring us to a prevalence of something.

Well, this is the fundamental point, the prevalence we are talking about is the understanding of the Creator.

Therefore love is a dual mechanism that at the moment of our reunion (the end of our evolution, the exit from Creation, the return to the "Father") allows us to understand GOD.

Understand that it is not therefore correct to say that God is love, as many religions do.

This is only a projection of the human mind for the self-complacent desire of a God-love, a good and benign God, even if there is no lack of a vindictive and terrible God in history, but these are also human ideas.

God is something that we will only discover at the end of our path ... in the right direction.

That is why it is perfectly useless to continue saying what God is and what God does.

We can only know this by completing our evolution and understanding love can help us along the way.

At this point it is opportune to talk about the symbol of Tao[95] again.

Love is also a mechanism that is enclosed in the circle of Tao, or better, in the sphere of existence.

Tao presents the concept of "balance" to us again or better still, the non-prevalence of one aspect over the other.

Love is the same thing, it has positive and negative aspects that mix with each other and maintaining their harmony is the best behaviour we can adopt to efficiently proceed along the path of evolution.

In this sphere, balance becomes the lubricant which allows us to glide quickly along the road of return to the Creator.

It seems almost to understand the statement of some ancient philosopher who said "in medio stat virtus": virtue is in the middle[96].

We could repeat it as "a fast path is a balanced path", what do you say?

One of the main tools of Creation.

In the chapter "Time and outside of time" I said a phrase that is very dear to me, in which I identified time and love as the two main tools of Creation.

"God gave us time in order to understand Him and love to rediscover Him".

In that page I spoke about Time, now let's see what I can add on the subject of Love.

The discussion is not easy because I am trying to express in human words and with human logic things that are beyond such terms, I am lacking an adequate "expressive modality".

I will try to at least get close to the sense.

Love is a "force" with a tendency towards union; when it has complete success at the end of our personal time, it will reunite us with the Creator.

---

95 In the appendix I give a more detailed description of the classical meaning of Tao according to Chinese Taoism: in the text I describe it in very reductive terms.

96 I think that this phrase comes from medieval scholastic philosophers, but the same concept was expressed by others: "méson te kai áriston": the best thing is the middle (Aristotle-Nichomachea Ethics) or "est modus in rebus": there is a measure in things (Orazio-Satire).

In this sense it is a tool that we have at our disposition in Creation to return to God.

It would seem obvious to think that being a force of union, it would have a "unitary" dynamic or it would be the pole of a pair of opposites which contrast in Creation.

From this point of view it is easy to imagine hate as its opposite pole, a clear force of division.

From this standpoint the good-evil parallel as the opposition of positivity and negativity and love-hate as the opposition of force of union, force of division would seem quite logical.

But the strange thing is, and here I have difficulty expressing myself, that love in its internal action in Creation has an ulterior dual dynamic, that it stops having only beyond Creation itself.

It is a sort of duality (love that gives suffering and pleasure) internal to another duality (love-union as opposed to hate-division).

The internal duality of love, the love-hate duality and the good-evil duality are the main tools of movement in Creation.

The complexity of their combined action in Creation and in humans is absolutely enormous, with the generation of secondary dualities which make rational understanding of the events of Creation impossible for humans and also incomplete for many spiritual beings of a high level.

Only spiritual beings of the highest levels have an almost complete understanding of this complexity, but it is a different type of understanding from a rational one that, in itself, contains only a miniscule interpretive subset.

I realize that what I have just talked about is only "blandly" understandable ... but I do not know how to express it better.

I am trying to render something understandable to our rational minds which we do not have adequate tools to understand.

If our mind cannot make it, we can get there by other means: with intuition for example.

But let's go back to the discussion on love.

Equilibrium in love.

I hope I have got the message across that love is the dynamic of Creation which intends to bring us back in union with the Creator, and therefore it is the most significant and important tool that we have at our disposition to evolve.

But to use it well we have to include its modes of operation that allow us to accelerate our evolution only if a series of balances are maintained under the dual aspects of love and other dualities in which we are engaged.

What does being balanced in love mean?

Maybe the best answer to the question is that everyone has to understand and follow their own personal balance.

It is not possible to give a general recipe because we are all completely different and at different levels of evolution and, as individuals, we carry with us a whole series of behaviours and previous actions (remember karma?) that make our path and our relative equilibrium an absolute "unicum".

It is difficult for me to say, for example, that a woman who is regularly beaten by her drunken husband and continues, despite everything, to love him, is out of her "love equilibrium": maybe that is exactly what she has been asked to do and what needs to be done in order for her to "grow" in the best and quickest of ways.

There is an infinity of examples and some of them could be terrible: maybe a ferocious terrorist responsible for a massacre is trying to return to a love equilibrium that he has lost for one reason or another.

There are really all types: these days much is being said about pedophile priests.

Their behaviour, which has been so stigmatized by the media, could simply be an attempt to retrieve a love equilibrium, for example a physical love that was negated by the rules of the sacerdotal path that they followed.

It seems extremely appropriate to remind ourselves that Jesus strongly advised us "not to judge" the behaviour of others.

Maybe the deepest meaning of his advice was this: abstain from judging the behaviour of a man because you do not know what is behind it; you do not know the complex mechanism of Creation, and especially the action of love activated in that particular existence.

We human beings cannot possibly know, because we have a very limited vision of what is behind things. Judging others is useless, in fact, it is counter-productive in the sense that it distances us from a correct interpretation of events and from a correct meaning of things: judging leads us to a mistaken and/or partial knowledge.

Let's limit ourselves to follow our own personal love equilibrium: it is the best thing we can do.

Knowledge can help with this. I was told:

"capture hate and go towards a love
from when you have excluded ignorance".

The fact of going towards knowledge and therefore excluding ignorance allows us to capture and stop hate or division and head towards "a" love which is union.

True knowledge helps us to re-align ourselves to the path of reunion under the action of love.

There is something particular worth knowing in the difference between good and love.

We often tend to make them coincide but in fact, they are two very different things.

Good like evil is a force, a dynamic but it is not an energy.

It is a polarity capable of attracting something, a type of force which attracts, just like the poles of a battery that attract electrons of opposites, generating electrical current (the movement) that transports energy.

In itself it is not an energy but a force of movement[97].

If there was nothing to move (to attract), good would remain there, immobile, doing nothing.

For those who have studied physics or engineering, I could say that good is analogous to an electric field, or better, a zone (in space for an electric field) in which charged particles are moved by the inter-action with the field itself.

Good, however, in its widest sense, is also a dynamic, or the convergence of more factors (not only the force above) that together contribute to the development of the action of good itself.

These other factors, which are difficult to define in clear terms, are for example, the characteristics of the attracting force, or better, the possibility of attracting certain things and not others.

---

97 The classical definition of energy which I spoke about in previous pages is "the attitude to carry out work", but work itself, or better, a force multiplied by a movement, is an energy.

There is also the way in which these things, once attracted, are made to work or inter-act with other elements.

Or, even more, they are the result of work of this interaction and address the subsequent use of this outcome.

I will make an example to try and make these vague statements a little clearer.

Good could be the request for help from someone who is suffering from a rare illness (force).

This request attracts a doctor (the particle present in the force field), a specialist in that rare illness, their interaction expressed through the verification of the presence of the illness, the research for the medicine and appropriate treatment, its application.

All of this allows a positive outcome for the cure of the patient. In turn, once cured, he writes a book on the illness that allows other sufferers, who would not know where to go, to be cured.

Good is all of these things together, a force and a dynamic.

Instead, love is only a dynamic, or more so, something which tends to make things combine in an eventual union, but without being endowed with any particular attracting power.

With this statement I mean to refute those who say that love attracts.

In the classic example of a girl who is irresistibly attracted by a boy, there is the first action of a force of attraction that is not love, that force could be good, for example, but it could be evil or another mechanism of attraction such as the conservation of species with a procreative end which, incidentally, is a kind of limited good in the material field.

Love could come into play and help the two lovers to unite, but hate could do the same with its objective of separation.

Neither good nor love are energies, the latter, if you like, are effects of good and love but other elements have to come into play for them to be activated (the particles in the example of the field).

The above statements can confuse us a little: if love is neither a force nor an energy, how is it that it has so much importance and ability to run things?

Well, I must admit that I lack the precise terms in the vocabulary of human knowledge that allow me to describe love.

Physics, as conceived by man, without the presence of the concept of force cannot describe the existence of movement.

But if love is not a force, how do I explain that the movement it led to is the most important of Creation?

I will give in for the moment, the Masters do not tell me much more, knowing that rational explanation is not within my reach, or perhaps that it is simply not possible to explain love with reason.

But I know what love is!

And you know as well.

In one way or another we continually experiment with it and its actions intuitively.

We try in a thousand ways to describe it but they are rather banal attempts of representing something that reason cannot recognize.

It is easier for us to live love and leave it to guide us.

That is the maximum knowledge that we can have of love: we cannot expect to put it in a neat parcel, if we try, then we inevitably reduce it to banalities.

Trust love.

It acts to bring us in union with the Creator.

Death.

Death does not exist.

Death does not exist.

This statement may seem strange to men who see the death of the body as the end of everything and as a consequence they are terribly frightened of it.

For the majority of men, death represents the first and most important fear.

It is an irrational fear because death does not exist and is only a mistaken idea in our head.

However, saying that death does not exist seems to clash brutally with the evidence of facts, everyday we see people who stop functioning physically through illness or accidents. Death is one of the preferred topics of many films precisely because of the strong emotive charge it produces.

So, if we have this evidence before our very eyes, how can we say that it does not exist?

It does not exist in terms normally seen by us.

It is obvious that at a certain point a physical body stops functioning, here we can certainly talk about physical death, but the concept of death should not be extended beyond that: the death of our physical body is not our end.

It should be clear by now that we are, in fact, much more than our physical body.

The key part of ourselves, in synthesis, what we call "soul", is something that lasts over time and still goes well beyond the short period of time granted to a physical body.

The soul, as it goes along its path, has more physical bodies (usually one at a time), which it "wears" and "removes" depending on its needs, as it alternates in reincarnations.

Physical life therefore becomes a "state" of soul, almost comparable to water[98] which, with the lowering of the temperature becomes ice and then, when the temperature rises, turns to liquid, in other words saying that physical death is the end of everything is the same as saying that ice melting is the death of water.

It is a banal and sometimes tragic error of interpretation caused by the limits of our "visual field", if we could see beyond the physical sphere it would seem just as obvious as the change in the state of water from ice to liquid.

The space between lives.

The Masters made me read a book called "The Voyage of the Soul" [27], the sense of which, summed up very briefly, is to affirm that *"physical death is simply an event that is part of the passage of a soul from one reign to another"*.

The author, a psychologist and psychotherapist, noticed that some patients, in certain mental states[99], spoke about events which seemed to belong to other lives; deepening the discussion, he tried to connect those events with the problems that the patient showed and to try to understand what was going on between those "past" lives and the present life, what is defined as the *"space between lives"*.

Given the consistency of the descriptions of his patients in a state of hypnosis, the author Michael Newton, an esteemed professional and atheist, is convinced of the "scientific" reliability of hypnosis, defined as a *"credible source of truth"*.

One of the key findings contained in the book is that many patients,

---

98   Goethe also used the paragon of water when he was talking about re-incarnation, he said *"What happens to a man's soul is the same as water: it comes from heaven and to heaven it returns, to return to earth, alternating eternally"* (quoted in [37]).

99   The memory of the events of past lives can be induced by putting the patient in a particular state of hypnosis, a process known as "regression in the past life".

recalling the death of a former life, declared their surprise and disbelief at being able to hover over their dead bodies, realizing that they were not dead as thinking entities[100].

He always noted in patients the "surprise of not dying", a clear indication that physical death corresponds to a continuation of our conscious thought activity.

Another significant finding is that almost all patients, after their death, *"leaving their body behind, feel as if they are back home"*, it is as if everyone understands that their *"true state"* is outside the physical body.

These findings are a sort of confirmation of the Platonic idea according to which *"when we are born we forget where we came from, remaining isolated on purpose so the experience of earthly life can be fully lived"*.

Newton also managed to reconstruct what happens immediately after physical death.

This has also been confirmed by recounts from those who narrowly avoided death, when they were dying they found themselves in a tunnel being guided towards a bright light.

This is all too similar to what the Masters asked me to do in the "voyage" I spoke about at the beginning of the book, that took me into a modified state of consciousness.

From this analogy we could draw the conclusion that the first phase of death is a stage that allows us to modify our conscious state, to access a different dimension from that of "physical consciousness" normally experienced by the living.

So going through a tunnel towards a bright light is a simple transition between two different states of consciousness.

The book, *"Voyage of the Soul"* goes beyond and tries to describe what happens once this phase is completed and one *"has entered fully into the spirit world"*.

Here the soul is welcomed by a personal spiritual guide, what we normally call a guardian angel who helps us through that experience.

Others are taken in by friends or relatives who have already died before,

---

100 This in fact is a practice in almost all the stories of those who have had an experience of "near-death" in which, apparently dead, then coming back to life and telling of having seen and heard everything the doctors were saying and doing from outside their body.

something that generally creates astonishment for those who thought that they would never see them again.

Here the Masters tell me that these friends or relatives correspond to souls that are not yet reincarnated, and also to souls who have already returned to Earth.

The latter, when the just dead soul is welcomed, have dreams or feelings in the physical body in which they feel a great closeness to a person that, even if they cannot recognize, feels familiar.

Voyage of the Soul then describes *a phase in which, again aided by a guide, the life just lived is analyzed, to see if it has fallen short of what the soul expected before it started.*

This process culminates in the meeting with a group of superior beings, who, instead of dispensing judgments, let the person concerned draw their own conclusions about their life on Earth[101].

Following this the souls are absorbed in the specific community to which they belong.

Do you remember the discussion of the "drawers" regarding souls, I did in the paragraph "Help from Outside?"?

Well, the home communities of souls is one of these drawers of "homogeneous" souls who are following a similar path.

Newton himself concludes that *"these groups of souls are very united and are composed of souls similar to each other, with common goals that work continuously one with the other. Usually they choose lives in which they find themselves as relatives or close friends during their own earthly incarnation".*

As far as I am concerned, I have not yet met any of those similar souls in this life[102], it is something which I expect to happen in the near future.

When you see two people in a very united and harmonious relationship, it is likely that their souls belong to the same "drawer".

It is great when a soul from the same "drawer" as yours becomes your partner for life.

Saint Germain said [30],

---

101 Here no one can "cheat", in this context there is a communication that we could define as "telepathy" in which a soul can not hide anything from the others.

102 In this regard, I suggest you read the book "Soul Twins Soul Mates" by Saint Germain [30].

*"When you free yourself of the idea that the soul mate is an entity
that can bring happiness, and when you want the rest of humanity
as a soul mate, then the entity - your soul mate, who will make the
experience of happiness possible - will appear on your journey".*

Returning to the contents of the book *Voyage of the Soul*, Newton also considered as very likely that *"people who are important in this life have been close to us in other past lives, hence the feeling that sometimes you seem to have known a person forever, even if you have just met".*

Newton inserted charts in the book relative to a grouping of souls and how they interact.

Another interesting aspect of this book is the analysis of the relationship between the actions that our body does in life and those that the soul would like the body to do.

The surprising conclusion of Newton, derived from descriptions of his patients, is that the *body and the brain often take precedence over what the soul would like.*

The power of human emotions can easily overwhelm the calm impulse of the soul, or consciousness.

There are no evil souls, it is often the human ego and the circumstances in which you find yourself that take over and drive life into a self-destructive vortex.

Nor is there a Hell where souls suffer for eternity, some souls who in life are stained by malice, are separated for a period of time from the main world of the spirit, for a period of reflection.

In some cases, the spirit guides work together with them, retracing the life just lived to see what went wrong, and to assess how their next life can correct the previous one, in the karmic sense.

The Masters tell me that this topic requires a significant investigation and invite me to re-read a text that I saw many years ago "Many lives one love" [37] and also invite me to read another book entitled "Life beyond life" [25].

I think this discussion will be the subject of some future book of mine.

Do you know how the Masters asked me to read that last book?

The day before yesterday I was in Lugano for work.

I was waiting for a meeting and was with my friend Vittorio, we spent a few minutes in front of some antique and retro shops.

After a tired look, from afar, at the shop windows, my eyes fixed on a pile of used books placed on a wooden box outside a store, at the top of the pile there was a pink and white book. Who knows why but for some reason I decided to go over and read the title of the book, *"Life beyond life"*.

Keep in mind that just two days earlier I had been writing this chapter, and you can then imagine my surprise in finding that book in my hands.

The coincidence was too much and I understood immediately that I had to read it, I was going to buy it when my friend told me that we had to go to the meeting, I left the shop, but the next day I bought it via the internet.

This is one of many signs that the Masters send me, organizing "reality" in a way they want it to happen.

It is a kind of continual miracle that never ceases to amaze me and fill me with joy.

In a little while I will speak in more detail of these signs and why I just can not believe that it is simply coincidental.

Union and the path.

From what I have said in the preceding pages it should have become clear that the aim of our soul and, more generally, that of Creation is the final re-union in the Creator obtained through the completion of a voyage of knowledge and experience in the duality of Creation.

Union is therefore our final objective.

But it is a little like as the "tendency to the limit" in a mathematical function, it is something that we will reach in the end, after a virtually "infinite" path.

In contrast, however, in the mathematical function the limit can be clearly identified, but for us the Limit-Creator is unknowable until we get there.

It is therefore perfectly useless to define the Creator, we only know that He exists[103] and that one day we will be reunited in Him.

That must be enough for us.

Instead, it makes a lot of sense to investigate the path that brings us back to Him, the path in which we are all up to our eyes in.

Some call it the Way[104] and also say that its main feature is its mutability.

The Tao Te Ching [12], the basic text of Chinese Taoism, begins:

> *"the true Way is really not a constant way"*.

---

103 I do not know if you can say that the Creator "exists", at least in logical terms in which we normally consider 'existence'.

104 Tao means "Way", also see the related appendix at the end of this book.

This aspect of the extreme mutability of the true path, the Way, I always intuitively felt to be very true, so much so as to be a guide to my behaviour.

In fact, in my private life, I have rarely defended my position by denigrating that of my opponent[105], with the conviction that what I considered true and correct at that time, could change and get closer to what the opponent said, perhaps with only the contribution of some new information or ... the turn of events.

The most appropriate thing we can do, given that the Way still has to be covered, is to make it as pleasant as possible and ensure that its length is as short as possible, since the Goal is our real objective.

Which translates as understanding what is the best way to live this existence.

Of course there is no religion or human group that has not had an opinion on how best to live and, perhaps, has also forced others to adjust to it.

The problem is that ... almost nobody has the correct opinion.

Or better, there have been some men of real value or truly Elected from Heaven who have included many aspects of the path and tried to pass them on to others, but their following was limited or, if there was a great one as happened to the Christian or Islamic religion, that which came after was not the initially correct indication, but its re-workings that profoundly altered its meaning[106].

How do we orientate ourselves?

Let's concentrate on the path.

Above all we have to understand that "living well" means living in accordance with the achievement of the final objective, the Goal.

---

105 This does not mean that I do not defend my position with stubbornness, at least until I am aware of its inadequacy.

106 Here I am reminded of a book I recently read "Misquoting Jesus" [5], in which one tries to understand the congruence with the original source of the writings that currently are part of the Christian religion. The result is that it does not leave much doubt that what we read today is something substantially different from what Jesus said and what the first writers of the Gospels wrote. In the appendix I talk about the synopsis of the presentation of the quoted text.

It is only that, not knowing the Goal well, means that we have to simply concentrate on the path.

I am an avid mountaineer and I know that the most compelling, and I would say, the nicest part of a walk is the walk itself, but it must be well planned and studied before, unless we want to have some nasty surprises.

I have to first investigate whether the path that I am going to do is within my capabilities, I evaluate its length and difficulty, I rate the route, analyze the weather conditions, I choose the right equipment ... there is essentially a phase of preliminary knowledge that allows me to enjoy the walk to the full.

For the Way it is the same thing: if we face it without adequate knowledge we are in danger of slipping, breaking a leg, being struck by lightning or doing damage ... no fun at all.

Accurate knowledge of the situation, however, cannot allow us to enjoy ourselves only, but also to reach the top of the mountain faster, since we have had no hitches along the route.

Knowledge, indeed, correct knowledge!

The purpose of this book, indeed of the series of books I am writing, is this, to reach a proper understanding of the path, its mechanisms and its risks.

It is only that, from my limited point of view, I cannot see all this route, and I risk not understanding all its important aspects. The help of a High Vision, that of my dear Masters, is what allows me to overcome my big limit.

It is a little like having a satellite which photographs the entire path from the base to the summit of my walk.

In this book I have shown you and I will continue to show you some of these "photos" with the "resolution" that I have managed to capture through the tools made available to me.

Maybe the resolution is not the best, but it already seems quite good and then ... I will try to improve it along the way.

Anyway, I am not the only one to have "captured" something.

There are some illustrious texts that show many substantially correct aspects of the path, while others are only partially true, and others still are wandering around in the absolute fog.

A good book, that the Masters advised me to read is "*The Book of Chuang Tzu*" [8].

This is also one of the most important texts of Taoism.

The extreme synthesis of the message contained is that *"the best life possible is that which conforms to the invisible universal order, the Tao"*.

That is to say that Creation is governed by a variety of mechanisms, including love, the conflict between good and evil, time ... that together generate some kind of *"invisible order"*.

If we could manage to train ourselves to it, or remain in that "balance" that I described above, we would live in the best possible way.

We will go along the Way on the right road without wasting time in the side streets that could be clogged with traffic and where it is more likely to have accidents.

The author makes it clear that once men had *"knowledge of Tao"*, but then that was lost. This statement is perfectly in tune with what the Masters have been saying for some time, or that signs of correct knowledge can be found in the past, and in my second [3] and third book [4], they made me pursue these signs.

Chuang Tzu defines Tao as *"the fundamental order of the universe, the way everything moves naturally"*.

If we want to live in the best way *(he says, to be wise) "we must be aware of this force that moves the world and keeps us in harmony with it, remembering always that it is the source of everything"*.

The above, according to the Masters, while creating a little confusion and overlapping between the Creator and the dynamics of Creation, we are essentially in a sphere of correct knowledge.

Among other significant things that the book says, is that the presumption of human knowledge is one of the reasons that misaligns us to the Tao.

It shows us the example of a *"scholar completely absorbed in its doctrines who will never begin to have a real understanding of the Tao, having some notion of Taoism, might make him think he is superior, but even that would be grounds for failure to be in harmony with the Tao"* [7].

In this we see a need for humility before the Tao, something which the Masters have always asked me to do, abandoning personal pride and human knowledge.

The Masters always reminded me of the broad Vision. In the book of Chuang Tzu it is said that *"we must keep our minds focused on the whole"*, or that *"the harmony of the Tao allows the recognition of life in its entirety, and not just the parts of it that we prefer"*.

The sense of wholeness ("my" broad Vision) allows us to free ourselves from a lot of unnecessary concerns, such as those concerning *"the cycle of birth and death, good or bad fate"*.

So we have such behaviour, that today we might call less stressed because we do not have to *"chase after greatness or avoid negative things. Seeing everything as a part of the whole, we cannot be offended or lose our reputation, because our eyes have turned to something much bigger"*.

Previously, I spoke at length about the search for a balance (in love, in the relationship between good and evil ...).

This continual balance may make you think of a "boring" life, no excesses but also no emotions.

Happiness, however, is an emotion that we all would like to feel. Chuang Tzu speaks of our continued pursuit of happiness as the search for what you want, and this implies a constant state of action.

But he says that *"people in harmony with the Tao do not seek happiness"* because *"their true happiness comes from not carrying the burden which normally weighs on humans, a constant swing between joy and sadness, between glory and failure"*.

If we are removed from these extremes, we can live in a state of *"action without action"*, I would rename it "action without stress", in which our actions *"continue without being at the mercy of our desires and inclinations"*.

All of which means, essentially, that being in harmony with the Tao is a transcendence of the normal human polarity, of the more or less sudden transition between the highs and lows of the human race.

And this is perfectly aligned with the "walking along the blade" of the Buddhists, but also coincides with the long speech made by the Masters to me on "preserving a balance between good and evil", much of which I have already talked about.

I found many other things in the same book that had been transmitted to me by the Masters, for example, They clearly told me that my life was addressed to a quest for knowledge and not power.

Chuang Tzu says that *"a person in harmony with the Tao prefers a life of peace to one of power"*, they do not seek power nor, analogously, profit or they have no thoughts regarding self-interest to impede them; and this paradoxically, allows such people to produce excellent results in their work.

Another gem[107] contained in the book is that Chuang Tzu considers, who is in harmony with the Tao, *"out with conventional morals"* and says that *"if you need to think about virtue, you do not live according to nature."*

And finally, what could also represent a summary of this book, says that *"the person in tune with the Tao puts knowledge in perspective: they have the wisdom that comes from the perception of the totality of life and that goes far beyond knowledge of the learned"*.

Still on the subject of the "path", I remember another fine text that addresses the same topic but from a different point of view. I refer to the text by Gary Zukav: *"The Seat of the Soul: An Inspiring Vision of Humanity's Spiritual Destiny"*, a recent text (1990) [39].

If we were to summarize the message of the book, in very few words we could say that it invites us *"to let our soul, rather than our personality, guide our lives, it is the only way we will be able to reach our authentic power"*.

This discussion connects well with what we have said so far, because it invites us to listen to that part of us, our soul, which has both a temporal continuity, much greater than that of the personality that is tied to a single incarnation and it has the tools to connect us to those who can transmit information with the broad Vision which we spoke about.

In fact, you should have realized by now that is not our personality that goes along that great path that we are asked to take, but our soul.

Our various personalities intervene in small fragments of the total path, and we need them to understand and experience the single or few elements of knowledge. It is not the personality, therefore, that is the "cable carrier"[108], the "backbone" of our voyage, but the soul!

And it is therefore the soul that must interest us most. Zukav says that *"the real purpose of human existence is the health of the soul"*.

He came to that conclusion after analyzing the lives of many extraordinary characters and realizing that their real power comes from

---

107 It is a gem for me, because I always had a strong dislike for everything that is convention.

108 ... excuse the infiltration of my engineering culture.

something that is *"beyond personality", they were all able to connect their souls to their aims in life* [7].

Zukav invites us to understand what real power is starting from the concept of evolution.

What does it mean to say that a being is very "evolved"? Was Jesus, for example, ... more evolved than Berlusconi[109]?

Jesus had great power ... what he did, his words and actions became stronger than the power of the Roman Empire, but he had no apparent power, Berlusconi by contrast, has a lot of apparent power: he has an enormous economic control, which also means an equally great political control.

However, I believe that no one can say that Berlusconi is more advanced than Jesus.

Zukav distinguishes between a power in the material world, linked to the five senses, the ability to control the environment and the economy, a fact aimed at the purpose of controlling others, and a genuine power that instead, is internal to the person.

Basically there is an external power connected to our personality, while there is another internal, that is connected to our soul.

Zukav says:

"the perception of power as an external subdivides our psyche; be it the psyche of the individual, the community, the nation or the world".

That, said in our terms, means that external power tends to division, or that it has a dynamic similar to that of hatred: a tool for splitting!

Conversely, internal power tends to union, the understanding of each individual event as constituting a unified whole ... the dynamics of love.

And the fact that external power is linked to the personality, while inner power is bound to the soul, can lead us to also guess that the personality, if allowed to, is addressed to division, while the soul, knowing better, is addressed to union.

By now it should be clear to everyone that if we are in the material world, then there must also be a meaning for the personality.

---

109 Berlusconi has nothing to do with Zukav, however the example I inserted renders Zukav's idea well.

We have still to highlight the importance of another type of equilibrium, that between personality and soul, which is to say between union and division, between external power and internal power.

And this is an uncommon conclusion.

Almost everyone is inclined to take a tendency to the extremes, some see external power as the only objective, because everything is focused on their personality, or there are those who see in internal power, in the soul, a unique end, thus denying the importance of personality.

This is also correct in the long run, but does not take into account that the path of the soul passes through many intermediate steps consisting of successive incarnations in which, through the use of personality, the soul acquires the experience needed to grow.

Indeed, we might even say that without personality, the soul does not grow!

Also at this point the necessity of balance has to be strongly stressed.

To anyone who negates the soul, the internal power, it must be said emphatically that that is the ultimate goal and therefore should be treated like a light that illuminates the path.

To anyone who instead negates the personality, it must be said emphatically that it is a sacred instrument without which the soul cannot move forward.

During incarnation the key word is always balance.

Remember the chart that I mentioned a few pages ago about to have/ to be, good/evil?

I will show it again below, but this time referring to the ratio of personality to soul and external power/internal power and you can see it is easier to understand.

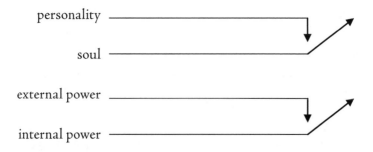

During earthly existence, personality and soul, as external and internal power flow along parallel paths, until they reach the physical death of the person, the personality and external power then undergo a clearly understandable interruption, the arrow points downwards.

While at this stage the soul and internal power assume greater importance, the arrow points upwards.

But, note well, the arrow does not rise vertically, but inclines upwards, meaning that there is an increase in importance and net dominance compared to personality and external power, but it is still not an "absolute" growth.

If it was, if there was an arrow pointing up vertically, it would mean that the soul would have definitely dominated the physical world, the personality: that will happen, but only at the end of its time, when the succession of incarnations will have made it grow (evolve) beyond a certain level.

But, for now, it is useless to concern ourselves unnecessarily about that.

Going back for a moment to Zukav's text, he also identifies a kind of equilibrium that is to be attained, what for me is a balance between personality and soul, he sees as a balance of personality itself.

The passage in which he says the following is very significant:

"When a personality is in full balance, you can not see where it ends and where the soul begins. This is a complete human being".

I cannot see this kind of fusion that he identifies, but I think it is proper to maintain the distinction between the soul which is our actual "channel carrier" and personality which is a simple tool connected temporarily to the soul itself.

It's a bit as it were, with a simple analogy, that the soul is the body, while the personality is a suit.

A beautiful suit that fits perfectly to the body, and makes it more beautiful and meaningful and perhaps allows the body to do things that with a less elegant suit would not have been possible or would not feel comfortable doing.

But we would never dream of imagining a fusion between body and clothing.

At the same time, however, clothes are essential for the body, because without them the body itself could not, for example, go out and show itself among other bodies, and gain experience with them.

The body needs the suit, but it is not the suit in itself: it is much more.

We could also say, like Zukav, that the body has a beautiful suit and is "dressed" so well to make it almost impossible to tell where the suit ends and the body begins ... but that does not make us forget that the suit and the body are two distinct things.

What Zukav defines as a *"complete human being"* I put in parallel to that of finding a "suit that fits very well".

That, said in the language of the soul, means that the personality of that human being is such as to adapt perfectly to the needs of his soul or is able to align its needs with experience in the physical world and to face these experiences correctly.

The latter aspect may, however, detach itself from the analogy of "finding a beautiful suit", or the adequate personality for that soul might not appear so beautiful on the outside and could perhaps even be involved in situations that are quite heavy and annoying.

From the outside we could also say of someone who does not have a good life, but despite that, that life might just be the most appropriate for that soul (a suit that is flattering, but not "beautiful"), or that human being could be "as complete as possible" in relation to the demands of his soul.

For this to happen, it is clear that the personality must somehow feel and experience the demands of its soul.

Even Zukav, analogous to what we have done and said at length in some of the pages of this book, sees "intuition" as an instrument to hear the soul.

"Because of our normal practice of experiencing only through our five senses, we are not inclined to treat intuition as a true form of "knowledge", what it normally transmits to us is undervalued and treated as a curiosity."

Instead it would be more appropriate to understand that insights and predictions are connected with a superior and wider mind, which knows more than what we normally know and is probably *telling the truth.*

Among the suggestions he offers for receiving and cultivating intuition, one seemed significant to me, also in relation to what the Masters told me.

Intuition[110] is aided by *"having faith in the fact that what we are experiencing in life has a reason, and trust that it is all for a good purpose"*. *"This makes us less ready to judge and more open to the truth"*.

Zukav says that *"intuition is like a walkie-talkie between the personality and soul. Most people do not want to trust their intuition because it sometimes shows us a path we do not like, a path fraught with obstacles.*

But if we are unwilling to follow the advice of our soul, we will never be able to flourish and realize our true potential."

The Masters say They do not agree much with the conclusions of Zukav, They criticize the fact that it is not a matter of flourishing or realizing a "true potential", but the fact of making the more correct path and as fast as possible for the needs of the soul.

Our personalities could flourish in many ways and have many true potentials to achieve, but the soul is only interested in something very specific.

The Masters praise the work of Zukav when he shows that the true power of a person (it is different from person to person) is reached when the person acts in the physical reality of doing things that the soul suggests and in the way it wishes.

And this only happens if the person is able to communicate and align with his soul.

The best path that we, personally, can follow is that laid down by our soul.

---

110 Talking about intuition and its importance in relation to other paranormal faculties, I am reminded of a phrase of Omraam Aïvanhov Mikhael: *"the intellect and heart are two faculties that are both essential for us, but they will never give us the true intelligence of life. To have the true intelligence of life, a third option needs to be developed, intuition, which is both an understanding and feeling. But be careful not to confuse intuition with clairvoyance, which is less of a power than intuition. Why? Because clairvoyance does not go beyond the objective perception of the astral and mental plane. So you can see the shapes, the entity of the astral and mental plane, and yet understand nothing of what you see. Conversely, with intuition, maybe you do not see anything, but you understand things as if you saw a hundred times better, because you live them"*.

The meaning of signs.

This book is a continuous surprise.

At first I started to write without having the faintest idea of what I had to say, and then I was told to do the first part by talking in fine detail about the experience of a "voyage", then They made me make a list of things to describe that I was only able follow in part and then abandon to pursue topics that were not listed, such as love, union and the path.

Now, that I thought I had finished, I am told to speak of the interpretation of the signs ... and I do not know what to say!

I feel at the mercy of a marvelous "divine wave", whose movement I cannot predict ... I'm trying to adapt and accommodate myself to its mysterious fluctuations.

I must therefore speak of signs and their interpretation.

Perhaps the Masters are seeking to broaden the discourse on intuition and to make you and I understand how to use it.

This means, above all, understanding how to put ourselves in the correct "mental" framework to gather the signs that our soul and the "wider world" continuously transmit and then to grasp their correct meaning.

But it could also mean that there are "signs" that are not "personalized" like those described above, but that are aimed at, for example, the whole of mankind or the planet Earth in its togetherness.

Yes, They tell me is this is the correct way to engage the argument.

Let's start.

Personal signs.

As you have now well understood, this book and all my books that precede it are based on a constant dialogue with the Masters, spiritual entities of "a widened world".

Mine is probably a very unusual situation in which I was used to perceiving signs of various kinds and with different methodologies, depending on what I am called to do.

From my experience however I can draw on some cases that are significant for everyone, as indicators of the "criteria" that the wider world uses to communicate with the personality of men.

I will show an immediate example that happened just yesterday.

You should know that the Masters have long insisted on the fact that this book and previous books, not yet released, should try to attain a certain readership, and should be published in English.

I am already getting Paola, the lovely fourteen year old daughter of my dearest friend, to translate part of the third book, but the Masters warned me long ago that she would translate only a part of my writings, and that there would be someone else to help me with the bulk of the translation.

But no one came forward and, on the advice of the Masters, I never went looking for the necessary help.

Yesterday, at a barbeque organized by my dear "witch" friend Paola, I met another friend, I had not seen for some time, Paul[111].

I shared a trip with Paul, an Italian-Scot, to Venezuela many years ago, and although he is very nice, we have not seen much of each other because we have two very different lifestyles[112].

Well, yesterday we got to meet again and talk at length about his work (teaching English) and something that I had never sensed before, his literary

---

111 I only notice now that I have named three people in a row named Paola or Paul ... is that also a sign?

112 If you do not consider labels and sayings to be useless and misleading, I would say that this proverb may be suitable for him "Bacco, tabacco e Venere, riducono l'uomo in cenere" (Wine, women and fags reduce a man to rags), in sharp contrast with my possible aspiration such as "in medio stat virtus" (virtue is in the middle).

passion for British romantic poets and his skill and enjoyment in writing in English.

I had never thought of him as a possible translator, but after yesterday's meeting, he seems to be the most appropriate person to do this: I received a clear sign from on high in relation to my need to find a translator and I noticed it.

In this simple example we can identify some characteristic features of a "sign":

1) The need.
2) The construction of the sign.
3) The sign itself.
4) The interpretation of the sign.

Normally we do not perceive the signs that life gives us because we are not aware of our needs. In the example above I have highlighted the need a priori and the link with the next meeting was immediately clear, but normally it is a little more complicated.

First of all you have to understand what a "necessity" is, it is a request from our soul, which is quite distinct from the "desire" of our personality.

Our desires, in fact, ardent and passionate as they are, only rarely coincide with the needs of our soul.

But earthly experience requires, first and foremost, the satisfaction of the former, sometimes putting ourselves in crisis because of the difference between personal desires and those of the soul.

The soul helps us to meet its own needs, but conversely it hinders us if we are pursuing other avenues.

Here another simple example could be the lottery, how many of us wish to become suddenly rich by winning the lottery?

A disproportionate number of people participate in the game, but the winners are ... very few.

Winning a large sum of money is a desire of the personality, we could make life easier (or maybe not) and more comfortable.

But the soul might not feel the same way: the difficulties of every day living, including economic ones, may be required to go along the path requested by the soul and to suddenly become rich would not give us the experience "required" for which we came to Earth.

In this case, the soul and what is around it does not help us win the lottery, and we will not win it, no matter how much dedication and persistence we have in handing over the ticket.

In some cases, however, the payout would enable us to undertake a path of change (... maybe giving away all the winnings to the poor) aligned to the requests of the soul and that is where we can win and in which the soul itself would endeavor to make us win.

However, the needs of the soul are fundamental.

And the soul tries in every way possible to put us in the condition to satisfy it.

It is no coincidence that we are born into a certain family, country, in the mountains or at the sea, if we are predisposed to certain diseases, or if we have a beautiful body or if we are disabled. Our soul has carefully chosen our body according to the needs of its earthly experience.

And the foundations of this choice are very complex, a variety of factors come into play including the type of soul we have, the degree of development within its path, the previous experiences that our various bodies have had over time, with any damage or positive acts that each of our single personalities has performed (karma).

But we are "placed" in a certain environment also according to the souls we have to re-unite with in an earthly sphere, and with whom we may have credit or debts of a certain type.

The complexity is enormous and is absolutely unmanageable in a rational way.

However, the gist of the discussion is that the soul has the need that our personality/body attains certain specific experiences and does everything to make us achieve this, the signs are the soul's attempts to move us towards those experiences.

We come now to the second point: the construction of the sign.

Our soul has a great responsibility in the choice of our individual body, and usually chooses it with great care, maybe waiting a long time between one reincarnation and another in order to find the "most adequate" body possible.

In this activity it has the ability to exert what we might call its "free will" or, it is essentially autonomous to judge what body is right for its needs.

Subsequently however, our soul has relatively limited possibilities to influence the behaviour of the personality in which it is inserted. It tries to continually send signs, but if the personality is not very sensitive in listening to its soul, the latter finds it very tiring to intervene.

Fortunately at this point, a lot of help can come from other spiritual beings, some give more and some less, they can intervene at different levels in organizing "environmental conditions" in which our personality is living.

Here it is appropriate to distinguish between two types of sign, one minor, which I will continue to call a "sign", which is given, for example, by our soul and that relates to our more restricted context, and one major, which from now on I will call an "event", the organization of which requires greater skills and opportunities than those possessed by our soul.

An "event" is such that it requires an organization of related events much larger than that of a "sign", for example if two countries avoid going to war that is an "event", while if I avoid a fight with my neighbour that may simply be the result of one or more personal signs.

Returning to the example above, regarding Paul, my future translator, spiritual beings made sure that a situation could be created where I could talk to him at length and "feel" that he was the right person for me, they made me go to that barbeque (which indeed I do very, very rarely) and they made me go to Paul, making me follow him while he grilled the meat, which kept him far enough from all the other people, I was encouraged to stay with him so that he would not be alone and in the end we talked about subjects that we had never discussed before.

The Masters, all things considered, had created the ideal situation[113] for me to understand the "sign" that he was the right person for my need to find a translator, and specifically it was not only my need or that of my soul, but also the need of the Masters, who were "informing" me.

---

113 Speaking of "event" in this case, given the interest also of the Masters in the affair.

Spiritual beings who help us.

Spiritual beings that help our soul and our individual body can be of various types[114] and are generally at an adequate level to the type and evolutionary state of our soul.

Often they are what we consider our "guardian angels", beings who have the task of helping our soul follow its specific earthly path, but there are other beings next to them, who may intervene continuously or on special occasions, these other beings have powers that are different from those of our angels and who help us gain specific experience.

Often the help of these beings is required by our own angels.

If we realize the presence of these beings who help us, it would make no sense for us to feel alone and abandoned, one of the most problematic states of mind of the human condition.

This topic of beings who help us is very complex and deserves a separate discussion, here I limit myself to illustrate my current situation.

I have two spiritual beings who are always close to me and with whom my soul has had a continuous relationship since time immemorial, they are not angels or spiritual beings that do not incarnate, but they are souls of my level of evolution currently not incarnate.

With them I had some moments of contemporary incarnation, in other moments of closeness where neither of us was incarnated, and other times like the present, where only one or two of the three is incarnate.

According to the Masters, I have "got up to" everything with them and we are very united.

We help each other, and when we are in contact, it is impossible to feel alone.

We are a sort of "Three Musketeers", "all for one and one for all", close friends whose friendship goes far beyond the barriers of the physical world.

It's a beautiful situation, which many souls have, although not all of them.

In this type of corporal-spiritual relationship, who is in the body gets

114 Even among spiritual beings there is a huge difference and hierarchy, they can go from being naive, ignorant and of low operational capacity, to being top-class, high purity and high possibility of intervention.

a range of benefits and aid from those who are not, but the level of such aid is equal to the development of our souls, nothing more.

This, however, is in the sense that prevents our personalities from making serious mistakes that can make us regress and helps us avoid problems with our physical body.

During life, we can have the closeness, even periodically, of other souls, maybe someone that we knew in the flesh and who then died.

In my own case I remember a closeness, that lasted for years and is now interrupted, with the last incarnation of the soul that was the personality of Don Leandro Comelli.

Don Leandro, was a good and spiritual man, he was the priest who married Maddalena and me.

His tragic death made the news which happened when thugs attacked him and set fire to his rectory.

I still remember him when I was a young engineer, full of trust in the infinite capacity of reason and he lovingly and warmly recommended that I look beyond that, because real life existed outside my head, no matter how clever I was.

I have always loved that advice, and if today I am writing these things then I probably also owe it to him.

After his death I considered him to be an angel, but now I know he is "simply" an evolved soul who I was close to for a time after his physical death, the Masters tell me that these days he is close to another person, a woman.

To evolve effectively, and our evolution also helps our friends' souls, we have the closeness of other spirit beings contemporaneously, who do not incarnate, and who are at a superior level to ours, but not too much.

These are what we call "guardian angels" and they are delegated, in the first place, for the conservation of our body[115] so that it can continue to play its role in the physical world, and at the same time they suggest the best things to do to evolve, but they have not yet had the opportunity to build the ideal environmental conditions to help us gain our experience of evolution.

---

115 For example they were the ones who warned me of the imminent danger of falling on Mount Blanc, in the story I told you about in the first pages of this book.

They can basically transmit many signs but they do not have the opportunity to build important "events", something we can do much more easily with our will power.

I have two guardian angels[116] who work together at the same time, they were entrusted to me at the beginning of this earthly experience, and they will stay close to me until its end.

I do not think that everyone has two angels, there are those who only have one and also those who have none, I would say that you cannot have more than two.

Their number is somehow related to the experience that we gain in this life and our need of protection.

In addition to the above, there are many other spiritual beings who help us at different times and for specific aims of our existence.

In some cases we can call upon them, such as during the "shamanic journeys" that I told you something about at the beginning of the book, or they may look for us and, at times, attack us.

At this point I can recall what is for me the wonderful experience that I am currently living through by being close to the Master and his Collaborators[117].

The Master is a spiritual being of the highest level, of whom I know little and I am not authorized to say what little I know.

I can only say that I understand that He has a very important specific mission to carry out on Earth, that is to put man, who is "skidding" excessively from Heaven's programme, back on track.

Through me, but not only through me, He is trying to convey correct knowledge to man, which is necessary to convince him to aim his own efforts and those of the human race in the direction desired by the Creator.

The Master and His Collaborators are spiritual beings of a much higher level than guardian angels, they have higher duties to perform and in doing so they interact with physical life in a very powerful and effective way and in particular, They have the ability to "construct" events such as, for example, my meeting with Paul.

---

116 Given the number ... you can see that I need a lot of help!

117 That's why sometimes I call him Master and at other times Masters, I cannot clearly distinguish Him from His Collaborator, or more beings together at the same time.

Their knowledge and power are vastly superior to those of humans, their limitation is that They are connected to the overall design of Creation, the evolution of the physical world and only partially to that of man.

Paradoxically, Their path of growth passes through man's, whose experience in his physical life "generates" evolutionary advances that benefit the whole of Creation.

It's a little like saying that we are all in the same boat, They are the captains, who give us directions, but if we insist on not rowing in the right direction the boat does not go forward or goes forward badly.

If man does not "row" well, at some point he will be thrown overboard and the boat will continue on its path without him ... but with a man down.

The boat will arrive at its destination anyway, albeit more slowly and with a missing element.

The role of the Master is to navigate the boat into port with all its crew ... His ability as commander also comes into play.

Spiritual beings like the Masters have a great opportunity to "construct events" and, secondly, to "construct a sign", which is the second point of our analysis.

They can give rise to events that are generally connected to our personal possibilities[118], linking people through seemingly random situations, or making someone have or not have certain experiences (someone saved from an air disaster because his alarm did not go off and he arrived late at the airport).

In the case of the Master the possibilities are so broad as to be able to involve physical individuals and events that affect multiple parts of the Earth at the same time and to make more spiritual entities participate simultaneously.

We earthlings could say that He has great knowledge and logistical ability.

But even He or They have problems.

As in all terrestrial situations and even in spiritual ones, there are

---

118 It is difficult, if not impossible, to make us win the Miss Universe contest if we are male and if we have a deformed and ugly body. If that happened we would be in the sphere of "miracles", they are possible, but they are not done if the effort is not justified in the sphere of the general "project" of evolution.

opponents and obstacles to overcome, the unpredictable changes in the conduct of those who previously had behaved like trusted collaborators.

Also for Them, acting in the physical world is not immediate or taken for granted. It is true that They can use "miracles" to facilitate their work, but this can also be done by their opponents[119].

The intensive use of miracles is a "forced" method of working that would oblige moving the field of experience (I would almost say the field of "battle" of Creation) from the physical one to a "super-physical" one and this is not what the Creator wants for Creation.

The Creator does not want "Harry Potter" style battles on Earth, even if we are forced to admit that they happened, they happen and will continue to happen.

So spiritual beings such as the Master, and also many others of an inferior level, are able to build or participate in the construction of an event and, consequently, make the sign arrive at its proper destination.

Let's go back to the "sign".

At this point the "sign" is evident in the physical world (point 3 of the scale), it can be an explicit happening, a special meeting or, sometimes, a simple but clear sensation in our heads.

At this point we come into play with our sensitivity and responsibility (point 4: interpretation of the sign) we can be distracted and miss the sign, or catch it and make it accessible to our minds, but then not give it due weight, or we can grasp it, interpret it, and willingly act accordingly.

The example of my translator is of the latter type, assuming he will actually do the translation[120].

The signs are of a more mixed kind.

Many signs are personal, relating to a deal that we are doing, or our wrong behaviour, or a well or badly placed affection.

Sometimes the signs are so small as to appear almost insignificant, sometimes they are exceptionally clear, accidents and illnesses come into this category.

---

119 We are in the field of white magic and black magic, see note 87 again.

120 Note that the English edition that you are reading was in fact translated by Paul.

I would say that if the accident or sickness is serious, these are signs of the "desperation" of our soul, which, after having sent us a series of small signs that go unheard or are misunderstood, has decided to launch a clear sign that obliges us to change direction (this is usually an incurable chronic disease) or, at worst, a sudden disease or a fatal accident, to interrupt the life of a personality that is so obstinate in not understanding the suggestions of his soul.

Chronic and/or serious accidents are not a coincidence, but a precise result of disharmonious behaviour regarding the needs of the soul that has continued for a long time in this life and, more often than not, even in previous lives.

Less serious diseases, that are usually curable, are also a sign of our wrong behaviour but also, sometimes, an opportunity to gain knowledge or experience.

If the illness is sign of wrong behaviour, our soul is giving us the chance to intervene and modify it.

In addition to personal signs, there are also more general ones, aimed at groups of people, entire nations or to the whole human race ... and beyond.

A war[121] between two peoples (limit sign) is often preceded by many signs that warned of its specific risk if certain behaviour was not changed, there are similar signs for the emergence of large companies or for the birth or fall of empires.

But a proliferation of signs can occur close to natural disasters, which are the same for the Earth as serious illnesses are for humans.

In these cases, the correction desired by the sign can only occur if, in the sphere of the groups of people interested in it, a sensitivity and a change of course is developed in a large percentage of individuals.

This is the so-called critical mass, that is capable of then moving to change all the groups involved.

For example, the signs of disharmony within the environment shown by the Earth comes into this type of phenomenon, if a substantial number of people do not decide to change their behaviour regarding their relationship with the environment, the reaction of the Earth, at least for human life on it,

---

121 A war for a people, is the same as an accident for an individual man.

will be inevitable and, if man does not disappear, there will at least be such a drastic reduction in numbers so as to create a new sustainable relationship between man and environment.

These signs are generated not only from the physical sphere of the planet Earth, as we normally think, but also by earthly spiritual entities whose existence we are often not even aware of.

Crop circles are very significant signs that, if we knew how to interpret them, could give us valuable information and immediate use.

These are more than just simple signs, they are real messages with disparate meanings, at times they are addressed to single groups of men at others to the whole human race.

In my second book [3] I widely, if not definitively, presented some interpretive criteria of the crop circles, I illustrated some messages contained in these manifestations and I showed how their content could relate to a variety of topics.

For example, some of them give messages that are relative to some historical happenings that have just come about and they try to transmit a deeper meaning beyond the immediate appearance normally identified by men.

Or they try to transmit, for example, the recalling of symbols that were shown to men in the past and try to reinforce the faith in those messages that ancient man had already highlighted.

There are still others that highlight serious "technological" or "scientific" mistakes that we are currently carrying out, others "ape" some of our most important scientific discoveries with the intention of letting us understand their huge superficiality and others still are warning us of imminent dangers be they wars or natural disasters.

But maybe their most important message regards the "mistaken" path that man has taken, with the intention of putting him back on the "right track".

This is the same thing that the Masters are telling me in their attempt to make me understand it and pass it on to you.

The crop circles are therefore a set of signs-messages that do not only have the aim of "creating" news and amazing an incredulous man facing such mysteries, the most important meaning is to make us understand things and to realign ourselves to the sense of our presence on Earth.

The problem, as for all the types of signs, is that we have to notice the presence of certain needs that the signs refer to and eventually correctly interpret them and decide to behave according to the directions they show us.

It is really not easy given that man is so obstinate as to believe only what he can see with his own eyes and cannot manage to see beyond that.

Unfortunately St Thomas is the clearest prototype of current man, this man, unless he finds the equivalent of a Jesus who obliges him to touch the wound in his ribs, will not believe in what could be his salvation.

My task.

I asked the Masters if I could now consider this book to be finished.
They said no.
However I do not know what else I can talk about.
So I asked the Masters to give me an indication of what the topic of
the next chapter is by quoting a line of a verse from the Bible [1] (Italian
version).

I was directed to the New Testament, page 235, second column, 13th
line from the bottom excluding the headings.
It reads:

> *"it has not been possible for me. My task is to".*

The first part of the sentence does not concern me.
The second is absolutely "clear", I have to speak about "my task" in this
story that I am experiencing.
Perhaps this chapter is meant more for me, to allow me understand how
to act and adapt to my destiny and the will of the Masters, but I think it
could be of interest for you too, since I was asked to write it[122].
Let's go a little bit deeper with the discussion.

---

122 Just today, while travelling in the car to work, I heard a phrase from Pasolini on
the radio, (I have not checked whether it's his own) in which, discussing the value
of books, he said that *"a book can serve the reader if it first serves the writer who wrote
it"* (I hope I have successfully captured the sense although I'm not sure about the
correctness of the quotation). Having heard that quote is a definite sign for me,
another fine example of how signs appear. And every time I realize that I have

On more than one occasion, the Master showed me some peculiar aspects of my destiny.

One of the times that moved me most and when I felt His loving closeness, was when, as I have said in my previous books, I received a letter from Him through A.

The letter had a profound effect on me, this is the most meaningful part:

"To Franco

                  I have followed you for many years,
                  I want to have you in front of me
                  and to offer you the shield of
                  defense from which you come.
                  Recycle your possibilities,
                  but that one be here
                  ●

For reasons of karma you will not need to live in difficulty to learn.
Avoid any errors so as not to recycle new reincarnations.
In a process of acceleration, that we are proposing, you can be sure
not only to heal your past lives, but also to discover why you should
not struggle with some aspects of common life that are more difficult
than useful for the understanding of human mechanisms.
We propose tolerance and well-being if ... you manage to shake
off the parameters and ways of thinking that are active in stopping
you from encountering what would be far more useful.

        ... and to you
            now be given the
                knowledge that you manage
                with love".

Faced with this letter all my hesitations collapsed and I knowingly accepted the great gift that I was given, a gift that is somehow part of my destiny.

---

received a sign my heart jumps with joy, it gives me the confirmation that someone is speaking to me from on High.

At first I did not say anything about this letter, I was afraid that if I talked about it I would be taken for a madman with a screw loose.

But then, by dint of direct and indirect confirmations, I was convinced that my prudence was just a form of false modesty, trying to get other people to accept me as a normal and balanced person.

If my fate is special, I must face it without hiding it, most of all from myself.

They tell me I am part of a group of souls with a particular task, to live with and develop a special sensitivity in the sphere of knowledge in general and, more particularly, true knowledge.

The idea that this was one of my peculiarities is something I have always had, and was especially reinforced when, along with A, I went digging into my past incarnations[123].

In more lives, I had the role of a scholar starting, from the years in which Jesus lived when I was a Greek philosopher-historian, not to mention the years around 1100-1200 AD when I was close to the Templars and for whom I addressed various aspects related to higher knowledge, or in the years around 1450-1600 AD when I was a learned man becoming an adviser to the English royal court.

Knowledge seems to be a continuous characteristic trait in the path of my soul and is part of my destiny.

There is in me a special stimulus to deepen the sense of things, to their most basic aspects, by trying to prune everything that is superficial, secondary, corollary, trivial and unnecessary.

I have an innate kind of annoyance, an idiosyncrasy I would say, towards what wastes time in vain, towards everything that is insubstantial.

I have been aware of this for many years and I am convinced that the reason I became an engineer is because it is essential to go to the "nuts and bolts" of the problem.

Sometimes this causes me problems, unnecessary bureaucracy, for example, makes me sick.

I also get annoyed by a large excess of rules.

---

123 In my first book [2] I talk about the partial reconstruction of the path of my soul in the sphere of incarnations on Earth starting from about 4000 years ago.

It is like I see an imbalance in the people who thought them up and imposed them.

This imbalance has then had repercussions in society and has become a widespread disharmony.

The "excessive regulator", as I call it, thinking of playing the "game well" by controlling everything and everyone has in fact played the "game badly" by causing a greater transgression. Paradoxically the more rules there are, the less they are respected ... and we Italians are masters at it!

Over-regulation is therefore the result of a poor understanding of the behavior of human beings, it comes into the realm of "secondary things" and is a "deviation" from the real heart of the problem which is a lack of true knowledge.

So my task might just be to "prune" the inaccurate and secondary things stuck to the tree of true knowledge, a kind of simplification and cleaning of that part of human thought that does not go to the deep meaning of things.

Now I understand that sense of annoyance I feel when I see the so called "entertainment" of TV shows, man does not need them, that idea of relaxing and having fun is a condition that is externally imposed and goes against our own deepest senses, it is living without life and is not what is expected of us.

This is another big point against the media and especially television, in general it tends to push man away from his own essence and keep him outside of what is really important.

And now the opposition that the Masters have repeatedly demonstrated towards all that entertains without making us live is clearer to me: holidays where you do nothing and get bored, reading the latest book of pure "escapism," spending hours in front of the television watching programmes devoid of entertainment, boredom in itself.

They are all forms that push man and keep him away from the "active" life he should live instead.

The Masters are against everything that keeps us away from the main aim that we are here on Earth for, to experience it yourself!

What I am writing clarifies many aspects of my personal life, I understand now why I can never stay still, why I have done a lot of activities and sports, why there is an innate commitment in me to do something, why I cannot stay more than quarter of an hour lying on the beach doing nothing, simply because I feel that my task is to live!

And when I realize that I am not living, that I am bored, something inside me rebels and tries to put me back on the right path and reactivate me.

It is only through activity[124] consciously created by ourselves that we can gain experience that leads to growth, this is the great sense of incarnation and the recognition of the great importance of our life on Earth as is absolutely necessary to lead to our soul's progress.

We should not be sleepwalkers.

The Masters made me read a particular book by Gurdjieff called "Meetings with Remarkable Men" [15].

I think that the Masters highlighted this for me because of the personal characteristics of Gurdjieff who, besides being a tireless traveller and an avid researcher of the spirit, was a very practical man and such a character is in perfect harmony with what we are saying in these pages, in which we reaffirm the paramount importance of facing the material life's challenges alongside the maturation of its spirituality.

For him it was *"necessary to live fully taking part in worldly affairs, but without getting stuck in habits that atrophy the mind"* [7].

He was always of the idea that *"an external environment of constant change was good for developing inner firmness of purpose"* and was convinced that *"most people in life are like sleepwalkers wandering around"* and that *"our true individuality can only be accomplished by questioning our habitual thought patterns*[125]*"*.

---

124 Let's be clear, activity is done both physically and mentally, so we need both to walk in the mountains or to write a book, seated comfortably, as I'm doing now. Boring ourselves is a "non activity."

125 The question of thought patterns is critical, for example, in shamanistic culture. To become a shaman, you have to get used to not using a fixed and immutable way of thinking even through heavy training and exercise. This is because a fixed way of thinking is a structural barrier, insurmountable for those who want to access dimensions which have modes of operation and logic completely outside the normal range. Within a certain "world" we can use frameworks (otherwise

The book's title refers to the relationship he had with some men he met during his childhood who were significant in his education.

For example, he recalls his father, who taught him to *"cultivate an eternally free space in his own mind and to develop an attitude of indifference to all that is normally disgusting or repugnant to others"*, an important teaching *"to observe without judging*[126] *and not to be a slave to his own reactions"*.

Of great importance in his education was the then deacon of the cathedral of Kars (Armenia), named Bogachevsky.

He taught Gurdjieff *"the existence of two types of morality: an objective one, which has evolved over the millennia, based on the goodness which comes from God, and a subjective one, which has evolved in different cultures, represented by intellectual and social conventions, and which tends to distort the truth"*.

Gurdjieff always remembered the *"monition from the religious man to live only by following his own conscience, the moral objective, the only one which can accompany us wherever we go"*.

The meeting with the Russian prince Lubovedsky was significant. They made many trips together, including India, Tibet and Central Asia.

From the prince he learned that *"scattered curiosity and jumping from one enthusiasm to another can be very counterproductive"* and may make one lose sight of their inner life.

The prince became a symbol of the *"danger of being too emotionally involved"* and formed the idea in Gurdjieff that *"a person must know how to balance thought, instinct and feelings within themselves, equilibrium*[127] *and integration of our various aspects are the goals of life"*.

Remembering Gurdjieff is a tribute to a character who sums up much of the guidance the Masters have given me during these last years.

For example, Gurdjieff's attitude of distrust towards the official sources of knowledge, like science, is extremely significant, it was *"unable to explain the many apparent miracles he had personally witnessed"*.

The main reason which stimulated his desire to travel was *"to experience*

---

we cannot work out the message received), but we must be ready to replace them as soon as conditions change.

126 Remember what was said in the preceding pages regarding the need to refrain from judging?

127 Remember all our discussions on the balance between good and evil, on love, on walking "along the blade of a knife"?

things firsthand," to the extent that one of the cornerstones of his philosophy became *"experiential learning: if something is true for you, it is".*

I also feel completely involved in his claim that says *"we must become our own source of authority".*

"Gurdjieff disdained the press[128], he believed they triggered automatic reactions such as shock and pride in the readers, a journalistic culture turns people into a pale reflection of the current mentality.

The average person builds a world that seems "real", but which is actually based on a filtered version of reality.

The awake, however, are able to see everything as if for the first time."

He, too, therefore, invites us not to be sleepwalkers but to wake up.

In our language it means that we must stop living life as made by others and to begin living our lives in the first person, Gurdjieff's message is fully in line with that of the Masters.

Friend of life.

I think one of my main tasks is really to become a "friend of my life".

There is a book I was given long ago by my dear "spiritual sister" Paola, I asked the Masters if it was appropriate to read it or not.

I was answered[129] that I read the first one hundred and forty-nine pages[130], or that part of the book which the Masters were in agreement with, as it would give me something real, meaningful and important.

The book, *"Anam Cara - Spiritual Wisdom from the Celtic world"* [28], it could be very briefly summed up in the following way [7],

"accept everything in life with a spirit of friendship".

The book is a meditation on living profoundly and is in stark contrast to everything that could be taught in a modern motivational course, it teaches us to get off the carousel of success and begin to really live.

Modern life, completely focused on the battle for success, to get

---

128 Who knows what he would think of today's TV?

129 Find the complete answer in my first book [2].

130 The number of pages is referred to the English version, "Anam Cara - Spiritual Wisdom from the Celtic world - Bantam Books - 1999 edition".

recognition, and also to achieve spiritual growth, implies an effort to *"shape our lives according to pre-made plans and programmes"*, in which we unconsciously suppress our potential for joy.

Doing like that we *"live a mechanical existence, without paying attention to our senses and to the seasonal rhythm of our life"*.

Our modern pace is based on the conception of a linear and steady progress, in sharp contrast to the Celtic sensitivity based on the circular motion of life according to the seasons.

This wisdom, in fact, loves circles and spirals and abhors straight lines, which is in perfect harmony with many teachings of the Masters who made me see the circle as the element of connection with the Creator.

In Celtic wisdom, there is no great distinction between spirit and matter, nor between time and eternity.

We live simultaneously in the physical reign and the spiritual one and therefore we are as much spiritual beings as earthly, we are "souls in the form of clay".

Anam is the Gaelic word for "soul", while Cara means "friend".

In ancient Ireland, these "friends of the soul" were often Masters or spiritual leaders with whom you could share your innermost self.

The book is about *friendship not only with other people, but especially with oneself, one's soul, with nature and even the idea of our death.*

When you accept everything in life with a friendly spirit, most things hold no fear for us.

Celtic Wisdom is also to see the eternal in daily life: poetry, art, friendship and love are just some of the ways that eternity is expressed within the limited space and time we call our world.

Eternity is all around us, trying to emerge and show us that it is a real thing, while the world we live in has created the illusion of being the only reality, we focus our attention on the material, impoverishing ourselves due to lack of imagination [7].

Since we are souls in the form of clay, our path to spirituality passes through the recognition of our earthly nature.

Celtic poetry, for example, is a vast celebration of the experience of seeing the mountains, feeling the wind on our bodies and the sound of waves breaking on the beach, a direct, personal use of our five physical senses, as opposed to the "flutter" of words or thoughts, that are almost always too dependent on what is external and thus can not constitute our true experience.

As long as *"we depend on what is external to us, our inner self will torment us"*, said O'Donohue, the author of the book.

The text attempts to represent a metaphor for the way in which normally we see ourselves.

We see ourselves as a crude fluorescent light, while the soul is similar to that of the paintings of Rembrandt, it gently illuminates and gradually reveals the mystery that it is to who looks at it.

We should admire with awe the mystery in every person and first of all in ourselves.

O'Donohue invites us to let our soul speak.

It is not doing stressful things that causes stress, but not allowing ourselves some space for silence, so that the mind can regenerate.

The soul is reserved, revealing its wisdom and pointing out the right direction only if we are quiet enough to let it talk to us.

Even if *"your soul has more sophisticated antennas than your mind or your ego"*, you rarely use them to *interrupt the chatter of the mind and allow what is true to emerge.*

Even Pascal told us *"most of our problems stem from the fact that we could not sit quietly by ourselves in a room"*.

Anam Cara also talks about the *need to integrate what we consider our negative side*, because it could clarify a lot within ourselves.

Maybe God wanted to tell us this too when he gave us *the commandment of "loving our enemies", by loving those sides of ourselves we have been taught not to appreciate* ... the enemies within us.

Certainly, however, *you must not exaggerate in the opposite direction, there is a difference between accepting your drawbacks and deciding to be negative.*

Our culture has become one of too much analysis, thinking too much instead of "only" living.

The worst kind of analysis is that mixture of guilt and punishment, when it is believed, for example, that God rewards us for the long suffering and for "carrying his cross".

In reality this is an example of how to throw the right of freedom and the right to the possibilities inherent in its nature to the winds.

Negativity is like an unnecessary wound that never heals, *trapping people for years in mental attitudes created by themselves.*

If the Catholic concept of sin had a sense[131], *the greatest sin would be a life unlived.*

The soul by its nature loves a risk, because taking risks is the way it grows.

It is only the ego that prefers perfection and to look for stability. Perfection in life is achieved only in the fact that it is fully lived.

According to O'Donohue we should think that *"there is no spiritual programme".*

One should not try to impose *any new practice[132] on our daily regime.*

A spiritual life is not lived to the full in terms of the number of monasteries visited or the amount of meditation practiced, but to what extent someone is prepared to abandon their fears and to give something of themselves.

O'Donohue's book has given me a valuable lesson that I have personally taken on as my task based on the indications of the Masters.

Its synthesis is an invitation to try to be friends with myself or a friend of my soul.

And, like any type of friend, I must devote time and listen to it, in the correct form.

Which, translated for our altered modern times, could mean simply *to relax and see what is special about normality.*

Affirming the importance of matter.

From this it should be clear that the Creator calls us to live life on Earth and our soul urges us to live as a protagonist.

The experience in physical life, in matter is therefore absolutely necessary, do not let any preacher of the spirit diminish its importance.

Without matter, our soul does not grow!

---

131 In a wider reality, it is clear that the concept is meaningless in relation to spiritual growth.

132 Here I refer to spiritual practices such as, for example, those derived from Eastern meditation. In my first book [2] I said that the Masters, at the beginning of my apprenticeship with Them, told me clearly to quit all forms of meditation or other daily spiritual practices because I needed to immerse myself fully in material life.

But, conversely, do not allow non-believers in the spirit to convince you that it does not exist or has no influence on our physical life.

Matter and spirit are obliged to cooperate and merge[133], that is what the Creator has foreseen for Creation.

My task is to say it loud to myself and to you.

---

133 Precisely in this lies the great significance of the merger between the masculine and feminine principles, in their symbolic meanings of spirit and matter. Here it may be interesting to go to review what I wrote about it in my second book [3] in the paragraph "Christ and Mary Magdalene, the cosmic union".

Appendixes.

Higgs's boson, the "God particle".

I will give you some popular information extracted from [12] regarding a subatomic particle that I mentioned in the text.

The Higgs boson is a hypothetical subatomic particle that plays a key role in the global theory of particles and, in this context, it is the only one that has not yet been detected experimentally.

Its name has been linked, since 1964, to the Scottish physicist Peter Higgs[134] who inserted it in a physical-mathematical model that he elaborated with other physicists in an attempt to resolve a major discrepancy between the theoretical model and experimental data.

In 1993, Higgs's boson, given its importance in the theory of the Standard Model, was nicknamed the "God Particle" by the Nobel Prizewinner in Physics, Leon Max Lederman [19].

<u>Premise.</u>

Scholars have long since developed a great theoretical framework of all subatomic particles, called the *Standard Model*, in which, like the *Periodic Table of chemical elements*, each of them is arranged on the basis of a number of characteristics that the model itself can predict.

---

134 The Masters tell me that it was not Higgs who hypothesized this for the first time and not even any of the physicists of his group.

In the sphere of this model, a large group of particles which act as force mediators is that of bosons.

But until about the mid-sixties of the twentieth century there was a serious problem, the model was not able to predict the value of the mass of single particles.

Indeed, if anything, the prediction was that all the particles, under this aspect, were equal and of zero mass value.

This meant that the fundamental property of the mass could be determined only "a posteriori" experimental investigation, thus creating a serious disconnection between experience and theoretical predictions.

In addition, the introduction ad hoc in the theory of mass values derived from the experience breached certain mathematical properties relating to symmetry, essential for the validity of the theory itself.

Theory.

To search for a simple analogy and to give those who are fasting from physics a rough idea of the contribution to the resolution of the problem given by Peter Higgs' theory, one can think of the players lined up on a football field for a game.

What unites them is being on the field and the chance to play the ball.

The ball and the pitch are therefore the unifying elements of the situation.

Also, before the start of the game, each player is equal to another in terms of skill, because if their abilities are not known yet, it could be said that a complete symmetry exists between them.

The playing of the game will allow everyone, depending on how they do with the ball and according to their ability, to differentiate themselves and acquire a certain value.

The next day the papers publish the form guide marked according to their performance.

Now it is a little as if Higgs had theorized a game of mass that had the particles as players, identifying the pitch, the ball and the rules of the game of the mass.

That is that each particle, which originally was without, acquired a specific mass value based on how they interacted with a particular new type of boson, and thus breaking the initial symmetry, as is said in physics.

Based on this mechanism, the theory of Higgs has allowed for a type of particle, bosons, to "see" the game, giving us the opportunity to fully justify the marks on the "form guide", that, in our case, are the experimental measurements.

The same theory also allowed for other types of particles, fermions, with different modalities, of indirectly knowing the conduct of game, and allow for less stringent conclusions.

It should be added that a prerequisite of the theory is that ball and the pitch can be found anywhere in the universe, including vacuums, and this would have made, and still would make, under certain conditions, the playing of the game an indispensible event for the particles (trust in this consideration).

There are also precise physical and theoretical reasons, but those are quite difficult to simplify, to which the acquisition of the mass in the manner envisaged would take place a very early stage of the evolution of our universe.

Research on Higgs' boson.

Each theoretical model may not, however omit experimental verification, and for this reason we require research on the Higgs boson, the recognition of which would be the final confirmation of the theory of the Scottish physicist, but at the same time, a good part of the great construction of the Standard Model, of which it is a fundamental element.

Currently the greatest hopes are pinned on the LHC (Large Hadron Collider) at CERN, the most powerful particle accelerator ever built, located on the French-Swiss border.

One of its tasks is precisely to re-create the same conditions of high energy of the first moments after the Big Bang, in which the boson would be present, according to the theory.

A particular description of the "God particle".

Leon Lederman, the scientist already mentioned, wrote a quite popular book [19], which traces the history of research, experiments and studies carried out by man to answer the age-old question "what is the world made of ?"

Within the text, often characterized by a unique sense of humor, he introduces one of the final chapters, "The God particle, at last" a text from his personal "Very New Testament" which I will tell you in full[135].

And She, the Almighty, looked at her world, and She marvelled at its beauty, She wept because there was so much beauty.

It was a world with only one type of particle, one force, carried by one messenger that was with divine simplicity, the only particle.

And the Almighty looked at the world She had created and saw that it was too boring.

So She worked out why, She smiled and cooled and expanded Her universe.

And lo and behold, it became cold enough to activate Her tried and tested agent, the Higgs field, which before the cooling had not been able to withstand the incredible heat of Creation.

And under the influence of Higgs, the particles sucked energy from the field, absorbed this energy and acquired mass.

Each grew in their own way, but not all the same.

Some became incredibly massive, some only a little and others for nothing.

And whereas before there had only been one particle, now there were twelve and whereas before the messenger and the particle were the same, now they were different, and whereas before there was only one force vector, and a single force, now there were twelve vectors and four forces, and whereas before there was an endless beauty and meaning, now there were the Democrats and Republicans[136].

The Almighty looked at the world She had created and was absolutely overcome with uncontrollable laughter.

And She brought Higgs before Her and, curbing Her hilarity, She chastised him and said:

"Why have you destroyed the symmetry of the world?"

---

135 The clear and complete understanding of the text is not immediate if you do not know all the background. Anyway I have shown you this excerpt of the text hoping, at least, to inspire you to read the book, seeing the humourous way Lederman has dealt with the topic. In the book you can see what a path of human knowledge is, it is often based on unique intuition that, thanks to the Masters, I now know comes from someone outside of man.

136 Here we see a clear American influence …

And Higgs, dispirited by this slight sign of disapproval, defended himself thus:
"But, Boss, I have not destroyed the symmetry.
I only brought out what had been concealed by the artifice of energy consumption.
And in so doing, verily, I made the world complicated".
"Who could imagine that from this monotonous set of identical objects we
would have obtained nuclei, atoms, molecules, planets and stars?"
"Who could have predicted the sunsets, oceans, the organic brew made from
all those horrible molecules agitated by lightning, and heat?
Who could have expected evolution and all those physicists pushing
and shoving and trying to fathom out what I, at your service, had hidden so
carefully?"
And She, the Almighty, holding back Her laughter, decreed forgiveness, and
a salary increase for Higgs.
Very New Testament 3.1

The Tao.

The Tao is a symbol that I have treated lightly in some parts of the text, there are some analogies in which I have only looked at few of its characteristics and meanings.

To compensate for this I have provided a description of the Tao quoted from [13].

Figure 3: the symbol of Tao.

Tao (道 literally the Way or the Path, in Japanese *dō*), often translated as The Principle, is one of the main concepts of Chinese philosophy.

It is the eternal, fundamental and vital force that flows through all matter in the universe, living or dead.

It is usually associated with Taoism, but Confucianism also refers to it.

In a word, the Tao "is".

In the traditional Chinese philosophy of Taoism, the Tao has the basic function of representing the universe. The latter, at the beginning of time was in a state called Wu Chi (= absence of differentiation/absence of polarity).

At one point two polarities of different signs were formed representing the fundamental principles of the universe:

+ the positive principle Yang, male, represented in white,
+ the negative principle Yin, female, represented in black.

The two principles immediately began to interact, giving rise to the supreme polarity or T'ai Chi.

The symbol commonly known as Tao is the most famous of many symbols that represent this supreme polarity[137] and are called T'ai Chi T'u.

It is important to highlight that in Taoist philosophy, Yin and Yang have no moral significance, such as good or bad, and are regarded as complementary elements of differentiation.

To describe the Tao, you can use the following analogy: imagine a person walking on a street, carrying a bamboo stalk on their shoulders.

One bucket is hung at both ends of the bamboo. The two buckets are the yin and yang. Bamboo is the T'ai Chi, the entity that separates the yin from yang. The street is the Tao.

The Tao can be interpreted as a "resonance" that resides in the empty space left by solid objects.

At the same time, it flows through the objects, giving them their characteristics[138].

---

137 I would define it as the "equilibrium of polarity".

138 Does this statement seem to have the same meaning of the behaviour of the "God particle" described above?

In the Tao Te Ching it is said that the Tao nourishes all things, which create a framework in chaos.

The defining characteristic of this framework is a condition of insatiable desire, to which Taoist philosophers associate the Tao to change.

The parallels between the principles of the Tao and the phenomena of modern physics are noteworthy.

For example, quantum mechanics show that the absolute vacuum cannot exist precisely because of the quantum effects of the universe, that in reality make it a swarm of virtual particles that can occasionally borrow energy from the vacuum to emerge in the observable universe manifesting themselves in the form of a particle and corresponding antiparticle (the two opposites) that immediately annihilate (annul) each other returning the energy they borrowed.

Misquoting Jesus.

Below is a synopsis of the book "Misquoting Jesus" [5] taken from the cover of the book itself.

How many of you know that the famous episode of the adulteress that Jesus saved from stoning by the phrase "He who is without sin cast the first stone", originally did not belong to the Gospel of John, but was added by an unknown scribe?

And that the last twelve verses of Mark's Gospel were added later to the original?

Such facts seem incredible and you would think they are glaring exceptions.

But they are not.

Errors, additions, variations and changes are the rule in the long and complex history that started from the writing of the first Gospel to the text that we read today.

Indeed, the manipulations were so common that the author of the Apocalypse threatened damnation on anyone who dared to add or remove anything to his writing.

We all think that when we read the New Testament that it should be, if not the exact words spoken by Jesus, at least those written by various authors credited with composing it.

The truth, however, is that none of the gospels we possess are the original manuscripts, and for almost fifteen hundred years until the invention of printing, the copies that were handed down through the Christian tradition endured countless vicissitudes, and were repeatedly transcribed by hand by copyists who were sometimes distracted or tired, sometimes uneducated, always, however, deeply influenced by cultural, theological and political disputes of their era.

Bart D. Ehrman, one of the world's leading authorities in the field of biblical studies, demonstrates that the more or less ancient copies, that have come down to us differ in a myriad of issues, some discrepancies are insignificant, but others affect the central nodes of the doctrine, for example, the divine nature of Jesus or the mystery of the Trinity, and are the result of changes, both intentional and accidental, introduced by copyists.

This makes it very difficult to try and accurately reconstruct the original text, an effort that has seen the involvement of numerous researchers, including Ehrman himself. [...]

Cabala and Torah.

Below there is a description of the Cabala and some notes of knowledge from the Torah taken and condensed from texts [14] and [15].

<u>Torah.</u>

Torah (Hebrew: הרות), once written as Thorah, is a Hebrew word that means teaching or law.

This term refers to the first five books of the Tanakh (the Hebrew bible, it is an acronym for "Torah, Prophets, Scriptures"), it is also known by the Greek name Pentateuco (*pente* in Greek means five and *teuchos* means book).

Judaism also uses the same term to mean Jewish Law as understood in a general sense.

More precisely, the word *"Torah shebiktav"* (translation: "the law is written") is used meaning the 5 books of the Pentateuch, or the set of 24 books of the Tanakh, and the words *"Torah shebehalpeh"* meaning the full set of codified oral traditions that came later.

The study of the Torah, as a compendium of divine instructions given to Hebrew, is one of the main precepts of Judaism.

According to tradition, every word in the Tanakh and also every aspect of the Torah that followed were given to Moses by God on Mount Sinai.

The rabbis considered that the words of the books not only provide an explicit divine message but are also the carriers of an intrinsic message that goes beyond their meaning.

In fact, they argue that even the smallest sign of a Hebrew letter was put there by God as a teaching.

An interpretation of Cabala is that the Torah constitutes the long name of God which is split into more words to enable human minds to understand it, but it is not the only way it can be split.

Cabala.

The Cabala or Kabbalah or Cabbala is part of the esoteric tradition of Jewish mysticism, especially the mystical thought which developed in Europe from the seventh-eighth century.

In Hebrew, Kabbalah (Heb. הלבק) is "the act of receiving".

The basis of cabalistic thought is the Hebrew Bible or Tanakh.

The secular exegesis of the Tanakh had for centuries placed the interpretation of the sacred text at the centre of life of Israel and the Cabala is inserted in this line of exegesis.

It dates back to the birth of the cabbalistic view up to the publication of the book Zohar (Splendor), published around the thirteenth century.

The Cabala is based on three main texts:

+ Sépher ha-Bahir
+ Sépher ha-Zòhar
+ Sépher Yetziràh

Sephirah.

The fulcrum of the drafting of mystical doctrines concerning the secret aspect of creation is a work that was probably composed in Eretz Yisraél in the sixth or seventh century, the Sépher Yetziràh.

In the Sépher Yetziràh, which deals with the secret forces of the cosmos, we find the first mention of a term that would become central in its subsequent explanations, the notion of *sefiràh*.

Literally sephirah or sefiràh (plural. sephiroth or sefiròt) means *"calculation, numeration"*. In the Sépher Yetziràh the term acquired a broader meaning, the sephiroth are *"manifestations allusive to divine energy"*.

Between the end of the twelfth and the beginning of the early thirteenth century, an extensive and already well organized literature on the mystical doctrine of the sephiroth appeared, and these were defined from then on as the *"degrees by means of which God acts in creation"*.

Virtually all the mystics say that they are in numbers of ten.

The names of the Sephiroth.

The Sephiroth also have their own names[139], Keter (the crown which is the fount of all the others), the highest and closest to God, Binah (science or knowledge) and Hokhmah (wisdom) at a lower level, Gevuràh (strength) and Hesed (mercy or compassion) at the third level, Tiferet (beauty) on the fourth, Hod (glory) and Netzach (victory or eternity) on the fifth, Yesod (the basis or foundation) on the sixth and Malkhut (kingdom), the closest to man.

Sometimes Gevuràh is called Din (judgment) or Pachad (fear), Hesed may be called Ghedulláh (greatness) or also Tiferet Rakhamím (mercy). Malkhùt is sometimes called Shekhinah (divine presence).

The sephiroth are represented according to a scheme called the "Tree of Life".

In addition there is also an "eleventh" (even if improperly called so) sephirah, Daath, which is collocated between Binah, Hesed and Hokhmah and represents the gap between Man and God.

The Tree of Life.

In the diagram of the tree of life the column of equilibrium that gives Kèter lies at the centre, Malkhut is reached through Tifèret and Yesòd. To

---

139 The methods of writing the Sephiroth found in literature vary considerably, here I use the more common spellings.

the left and right of Kèter two columns branch off, one of Grace, through Hokhmah, Hèsed and Nètzah, and that of severity rising up through Hod, Gevuràh and Binàh.

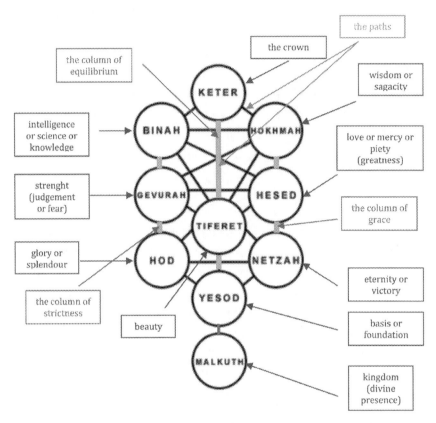

Figure 4: the Tree of Life containing the 10 sephiroth, the columns and the paths.

The twenty-two paths.

The 10 Sephiroth are connected to each other by 22 paths, associated with the Hebrew alphabet.

A number of authors have presented various types of association.

Figure 5: another representation of the Tree of Life, with the presence of the 11th Sephiroth, Daath, or the gap between God and man [17]. The main path of descent into matter and the re-ascent is in grey.

The most common starts Aleph (א) from Kèter in the direction of Hokhmah (Chochmah) and ends with the Thaw (ת) which is between Yesòd and Malkhùt.

The 22 paths and the ten Sephiroth form together the 32[140] ways mentioned in the Sépher Yetziràh.

---

140 By combining these 32 ways (in fact, I am told by the Masters that there are more), which basically represent God's mode of action in Creation, with the 38 guiding and catalystic principles as mentioned in the interpretation of the Zodiac of Dendera (see my third book [4]), we can reach a comprehensive understanding of the "ingredients of Creation and their mix". At this level of understanding, however, reason may do little more than bring us back to a simplified description.

The four worlds.

At the beginning of the fourteenth century they began to distinguish four worlds in Creation, *'Atzilùth* (the world of emanation), *Beri'à* (the world of Creation), *Yetzirà* (the world of shapes) and *'Asiya* (the world of production or manufacture).

With these names the variants of the type of influx of Sephiroth were shown.

The world of *'Atzilùth*, which is closer to God, is only governed by immaterial forces.

The material component gradually increases as it distances itself from the Emanator.

Correlations.

Although not visible to the eyes, the Sephiroth are perceived by the mystic, which rises from below to the supreme through contemplation and study of cosmic correlations.

All components of the universe have their correlations: the sun is Tifèret, Yesòd, the Moon, Malkhùt the Earth, and so on.

Even the twenty-two paths are combined, in addition to letters of the Hebrew alphabet, to the tarot cards, to the signs of the zodiac, planets and elements, etc.

The existence of these groups goes back to the gnosis and a magical view of the universe in which every part is connected to another.

This complex set of relationships reminds us of modern scientific theories such as that of chaos.

What is not knowable is that which is beyond the highest sephirah, that is the Almighty, being immeasurable therefore cannot be perceived by humans[141].

Emanations.

The question arises of how an Infinite Being, the one who Isaac the Blind first called the *En Sof* (Unending), could emanate aspects of Himself in a finite world.

According to Moses Cordovero [16] (1522-1570), Hebrew mystic, God contracted Himself in order to be able to emanate His energy in the finite world, and "show His glory to the people".

The contraction of God (*tzimtzùm*) is at the center of the speculation of Isaac Luria [17] (1534-1572), a famous mystic and Jewish Rabbi.

As a result of emanation, according to Luria, vases were created to contain the divine energy.

The supernal vases, the strongest, resisted the pressure of light well, but the inferior ones broke and dispersed the energy.

The fragments of broken vases still contain particles of light, these are the *Qelipòth* (shells), the forces of evil.

The Cabala of names.

The Hebrew word *tzeraf* denotes both the alchemic transmutation and the interchange of the letters of the alphabet. Hebrew exegetes were used to permutating the letters of the Tanakh to discover hidden meanings and more truths.

---

141 Reading these notes really excites me, the Masters, by making me interpret the Zodiac of Dendera (see my third book [4]), made me learn the same thing, the unknowability of the Creator. In that context, I realized that the Creator is unknowable by those in Creation because the guiding principles of the knowledge of the Creator are not incorporated in Creation itself, which is to say that the Creator is "immeasurable" because we have not been given a way to "measure" Him. Discovering that cabalistic knowledge came to the same conclusion (and I assure you I did not know this before) as that gradually handed down to me by the Masters, filled me with wonder, and reconfirmed, as if I had not already had enough evidence, of the depth of their knowledge.

The numeric permutation is called *ghimatréyah*.

Each letter of the Hebrew alphabet denotes a number, therefore each word of the Bible has its own numerical value, the sum of the numerical values of the letters that compose it.

A word can be replaced with another of the same numerical value.

For example:

AChaD in Hebrew means "unity" and is equal to 13 (A=1 + Ch=8 + D=4).

Even the word "love", AHaVaH has the same number (A=1, H=5, V=2, H=5).

In this way, as in an equation, we can say that:

$$AChaD = AHaVaH\,{}^{142}.$$

The art of *Notariqòn* allows the discovery of hidden words inside other words (the letters of a word as the revelation of other words.)

The cabalistic alchemy.

Already by the thirteenth-century Séfer ha-Zòhar alchemical ideas were found linked to the symbolism of the Sephiroth and the transmutation of metals.

The seven types of gold mentioned in the tradition becomes a metaphor of the seven inferior Sephiroth, while Binah is called "supernal gold".

How to and who comes close to the Cabala.

There are different approaches to the Cabala according to the attitude of who comes close to it.

The approaches also vary because it can be compared with all the canonical texts of Jewish tradition.

Given that the Cabala is the soul of the Torah, many of its basic ideas are spread widely among the people of Israel, among academics, religious

---

142 Do you remember all our discussions on love and unity ...?

scholars, or, at a higher level, among rabbis often endowed with mystical qualities, and finally among mystics themselves.

The latter two categories are men more prone to intellectual perception and mystical experience often associated with the manifestation of miracles.

The same prophets of the people of Israel have always been familiar with the innermost secret of the Torah and its close relationship with God.

In the messianic era, it will be easily available to all the people of Israel.

The essence of the Cabala.

The following is an excerpt from [7], which recalls the book by Matt [20] "*The Essential Cabala - The Heart of Jewish mysticism*".

Reading that book was suggested to me by the Masters as worthy of interest because it contains a knowledge and a wisdom superior to the human ones.

A way out of the darkness.

Despite having ancient roots, the Cabala was not discovered until 1100, in a community of Jews gathered in the south of France.

Later it spread beyond the Pyrenees, to Spain, while integrating some elements of Pythagorean mysticism, Neoplatonism and Sufi.

In 1280, a Spanish Jewish mystic, Moses de Leon, produced a body of writings that were said to have been dictated through a form of channeling.

The material was expanded to become the enormous *Sefer-ha-Zohar* (The Book of Splendour), written in Aramaic.

Originally it was a commentary on the Torah in terms of its interesting images, the book then became the Zohar as we know it nowadays.

The Zohar reveals that the Torah is a code that sheds light on the mechanisms of Creation, or how the world has emerged from the Infinite (called "*Ein Sof*").

The most famous of the masters of the Cabala was Moses Cordovero, whose book *Pardis Rimonim* (The garden of pomegranates) summarized three centuries of cabalistic wisdom.

His legacy was collected by Isaac Luria, or *Ha-Ari* (the Lion), which left no writings, but whose ideas had a strong influence on Hasidic Judaism spread in Eastern Europe.

One interesting thing is that the Renaissance philosopher Pico della Mirandola had read all the translations of the Cabala in Latin, and defended it as scripture that confirmed the divinity of Jesus.

The tradition of the influence of the Cabala continued with non-Jewish philosophers such as Gottfried Leibniz, Emanuel Swedenborg and William Blake.

What is the Cabala?

The aim of cabalistic practice is to bring a person to "cosmic consciousness", or mystical union with God, which humanity enjoyed at the beginning of creation before the "fall" into the knowledge of good and evil (symbolized by Adam and Eve).

Matt says the early cabalists, to reach this mystic end, had to stay very close to the teachings and traditional laws of conventional Judaism.

They remained faithful to the *talmud* (the fundamental body of law, history and Jewish customs) and to the Bible, expressing the traditional values of God and men, exemplified by *mitsvot* (the Commandments), but tried to add to and complete them by exploring the more feminine aspects of the divine (symbolized by the archetypal feminine, goddess *Shekhinah*) leaning towards a kind of mystical union.

Illumination of this kind could not be obtained through mere intellectual study, so a learning system based on the *sephiroth* was created, i.e. a map of consciousness that evokes every aspect of creation and people.

The ten recipients.

The *Sefer Yetzirah* (The book of creation) existed before the Cabala, this is a fundamental book for Jewish mysticism.

It told how God created the world by pronouncing a union of sacred letters and numeric entities, the ten *sephiroth*, which emerged from *Ein Sof*, the unknowable Divine Essence or the Divine Infinite that preceded time and space.

The ancient cabalist Isaac Luria sought to explain the beginning of the world and the meaning of existence through what he taught on the *sephiroth*.

Its conception was as follows: a light appeared inside the vacuum of *Ein Sof.*

The light began to pour into some containers or recipients of the spirit (the *sephiroth*).

Some of them could not withstand the force of divine light, and broke into a thousand pieces.

Most of the light returned to its source, but the shattered remains of the containers, in addition to the sparks that had been created, were imprisoned in material existence.

The task of human life is "to raise the sparks back" to their original divinity, which can only be achieved by living a holy life, everyday actions are considered as something that promotes or prevents the raising or return to the original form of the divine sparks.

Another way to explain *Ein Sof* and the *sephiroth* is to imagine God's light shining through stained glass windows, and that each of the *sephiroth* is an archetypal expression or a characteristic of God that can be found in Creation in general or specifically in humans.

Matt provides a thorough explanation of the *sephiroth* and how they can be guides for the character and lives of people.

We shelter some personalities inside of us that are waiting to be activated, the author postulates that people can become expressions of certain *sephiroth*.

Abraham was a man of Hèsed, Isaac of Gevuràh, Joseph a master of Yesòd, and so on.

Self-realization.

According to the Cabala, the divine realm needs human action in order that the world can realize its own potential.

Without us, God is incomplete.

On the other hand, it is up to us to reflect on the mysteries of God and Creation.

Matt quotes Moses de Leon when he observed:

"How precious it is to know that God generates all that exists.
From a small piece of existence, the soul can perceive the
existence of God, which has neither beginning nor end".

Frequently thinking of the vastness of God makes us humble and makes us the vehicle of divine expression.

Dov Baer, a Hasidic master of the eighteenth century, said:

"If you think of yourself as something specific and finite, then
God can not take your remains, because God is infinite".

The Cabala regards the realization of self, but the true realization of all our potential can only take place by "adhering to God".

De Leon argued that the soul takes human form because it is not complete and needs to be realized "in every dimension". The meaning of our life on this Earth is the fulfillment of a purpose planned by God, and the Cabala points the way towards the self-knowledge needed to discover this purpose.

The concept of "raising the sparks" simply means begin to recognize and realize the potential which God has endowed us with.

Endnotes.

Why is there always so much mystery around the learning of the Cabala?

Traditionally, there were restrictions regarding who could be given access to cabalistic teachings, for example you had to be more than forty years old, be married and have a strong heart and mind.

As these restrictions have been abandoned in many cases, the reasoning behind them is not unfounded.

Since they deal with deeper questions of self and of God, the Cabala tends to push a person out from his usual orbit of thought, and the masters of this discipline know that mystical knowledge can lead to madness, if the individual does not know how to incorporate it into their own understanding of the world. Regarding this point, Matt quotes Isaac of Akko:

"Now make the effort and strain to see the supreme light,
because I have brought you into a boundless ocean.
But be careful!
Strain to see, but avoid drowning".

The masters of the Cabala have never made an effort to find new followers, for the simple reason that it makes no sense to impose this kind of knowledge on those who are not ready to swim in these waters but, to those who sincerely desire to grow spiritually, the Cabala represents a very rich land of inspiration and guidance that does not belong only to Judaism, but to all humanity.

Bibliography.

The Masters have repeatedly said that the reading of texts whose content comes from the human mind is often misleading and counterproductive.

They have sometimes asked me to decisively ignore some readings and, in general, have encouraged me to reduce the time spent reading: "who reads does not write", in their own way they reminded me that my priorities were to write. However, in several of our meetings numerous texts, either positive or negative, were called upon.

The following is a partial list of the texts from which I have gathered some information, sometimes I have used whole parts or sometimes I have simply extracted images or photos.

I have not cited texts in whose reading I was strongly discouraged.

1] Various Authors – *La Bibbia (The Bible)*– Editrice Elle Di Ci – Leumann – Turin, Italy – 1985.

2] Alessandrini Francesco – *Voyage in destiny – first part – A private diary* – awaiting publication - 2009.

3] Alessandrini Francesco – *Voyage in destiny – second part – The diary of the development of my public story* – awaiting publication – 2009.

4] Alessandrini Francesco – *Voyage in destiny – third part – From the analysis of certain ancient discoveries, a message for the survival of mankind* – awaiting publication – 2010.

5] Bart D. Ehrman – *Misquoting Jesus* – Harper Collins – USA – 2005.

6] Braden Gregg – *Beyond zero point* – DVD (revised 2009) – Seattle Washington – 2005.

7] Butler-Bowdon Tom – *50 Spiritual Classics* – Nicholas Brealey Publishing – London and Boston – 2005.

8]   Chuang Tzu – *The Book of Chuang Tzu* – Penguin – London – 1996.

9]   Cioran Emile – *La chute dans le temps (The fall into time)* – Editions Gallimard – Paris – 1964.

10] Descartes René – *Dissertazione sul metodo (Discourse on the method)* – Agenzia Libraria Editrice – Trieste, Italia – 2007.

11] Doliner Roy, Blech Benjamin – *The Sistine secrets* – Harper Collins – USA – 2008.

12] Duyvendak J.J.L. (Editor) – *Tao tö king, Le Livre de la Voie et de la Vertu (The book of the way and its virtue)* – Librairie d'Amerique et d'Orient – Adrien-Maissonneuve – Paris - 1953.

13] Einstein Albert – *Relativity: The Special and General Theory* – Bartleby – New York –2000.

14] Givaudan Anne – *Formes-Pensées, decouvrir et comprendre leurs influences sur notre santé et sur notre vie (Thought-Shapes , discover and understand their influences on our health and life)* – Editions S.O.I.S. – Plazac – France – 1996.

15] Gurdjieff Georges Ivanovitch – *Meetings with Remarkable Men* – Picador – London – 1978.

16] Hancock Graham – *Supernatural. Meeting with Ancient Teachers of Mankind* – © Graham Hancock – 2005.

17] Huxley Aldous – *The Doors of Perception* – Flamingo – London – 1994.

18] Jung Carl Gustav – *Memories, Dreams, Reflections* – William Collins – Glasgow – 1978.

19] Lederman Leon e Teresi Dick – *The God Particle: If the Universe is the Answer, What is the Question* – Houghton Mifflin Company – 1993.

20] Matt Daniel Chanan – *The Essential Kabala: The Heart of Jewish Mysticism* – HarperCollins – New York – 1994.

21] Maurey Eugene – *Exorcism* – Whitford Press – Atglen PA, USA – 1988.

22] Melchizedek Drunvalo – *The Ancient Secret of the Flower of Light, first part* – Light Technology Publishing – Flagstaff, AZ – USA – 1998.

23] Melchizedek Drunvalo – *The Ancient Secret of the Flower of Light, second part* – Light Technology Publishing – Flagstaff, AZ – USA – 2000.

24] Meurois–Givaudan Anne e Daniel – *Wesak, il tempo della riconciliazione (The time of reconciliation)* – Edizioni Amrita – Torino.

25] Moody Raymond A. Jr – *Life after Life* – Harper – San Francisco CA – 2001.

26] Murry Hope – *The Sirius Connection* – Element Books Limited – Shaftesbury, Dorset – GB – 1996.

27] Newton Michael – *Journey of Souls: Case Studies of Life Between Lives* – Llewellyn Publications – St. Paul – 2002.

28] O'Donohue John – *Anam Cara, Spiritual Wisdom from the Celtic World* – Bantam Press – GB – 1997.

29] Pascal Blaise – *Pensieri (Pensées)* – Mondadori – Milano – 1976.

30] Saint Germain – *Twin souls & Soulmates* – Triad Publishers PTY ltd – 1993.

31] Schucman Helen, Thtford William – *A Course in Miracles* – Viking – NY – 1996.

32] Sibaldi Igor – *Il mondo invisibile (The invisible world)* – Edizioni Frassinelli – 2006.

33] Sibaldi Igor – *Libro degli angeli (The book of angels)* – Edizioni Frassinelli – 2007.

34] Sitchin Zecharia – *The 12th Planet* – Zecharia Sitchin – 1976.

35] Taleb Nassim Nicholas – *The Black Swan* – Nassim Nicholas Taleb – 2007.

36] Turoldo David Maria – *Amare* (To love)– Edizioni Paoline – Cinisello Balsamo (MI) – 1986.

37] Weiss Brian – *Only Love is Real* – Brian Weiss, MD – 1996.

38] Zolnerr Frank – *Leonardo da Vinci: the complete paintings and drawings* – Taschen – Köln – 2003.

39] Zukav Gary – *The Seat of the Soul: An Inspiring Vision of Humanity's Spiritual Destiny* – Rider Books – London – 1991.

Web sites.

A list of web sites that have been visited during the writing of this book follows.

I1] You Tube: UFOs making crop circles

I2] http://it.wikipedia.org/wiki/Higgs

I3] http://it.wikipedia.org/wiki/Tao

I4] http://it.wikipedia.org/wiki/Cabala

I5] http://it.wikipedia.org/wiki/Torah

I6] http://en.wikipedia.org/wiki/Moses_Ben_Jacob_Cordovero

I7] http://en.wikipedia.org/wiki/Isaac_Luria

About the Author

FRANCESCO ALESSANDRINI is a fifty two year old engineer who works on the planning and design of important civil engineering structures (bridges, roads, ports and dams). He taught for ten years at the University of Udine in the geotechnical sector and has published numerous articles especially in the structural and geotechnical field. His commitment and enthusiasm for his profession has not impeded his interest in subtle energies and phenomena correlated to the states of a widened consciousness, which started fifteen years ago.

This personal research has allowed him to deepen his knowledge in a multiplicity of sectors such as bio-architecture, geobiology, divining, radionics and shamanism as well as travelling widely and developing spiritual and historical knowledge relative to diverse populations of Earth. This increased knowledge and the subsequent development of spiritual sensitivity has allowed him to come in contact with completely atypical cognitive realities fundamental in understanding the meaning of the life of man and much more.

This knowledge underwent an unexpected and exponential growth when he came in contact with the Masters of Light of high level three years ago. Their help transmitted a series of knowledge on varied aspects of creation and on the life of man which has been transcribed into four books, all of them with the same title "Voyage in Destiny", as suggested by the Masters.

The books, which have not been published yet, are all addressed to the deepening of "true knowledge" or a knowledge that does not come from the limited human point of view, but which contains all the knowledge and wisdom of a spirit endowed with an immensely wider vision than man's.

The books deal with the following arguments:

Voyage in Destiny, part one	A private diary.
Voyage in Destiny, part two	The diary of the development of my public story.
Voyage in Destiny, part three	From the analysis of certain ancient discoveries, a message for the survival of mankind.
Voyage in Destiny, part four	The return to true knowledge.

Francesco Alessandrini is married with the sweet Maddalena; they live in Udine – Italy.